Michael D. Coker

The Battle of Port Royal

Battle of Port Royal Ferry, 1862.

To my wife, Sheri Ducker. Without you this book would have never been possible. As always, you sacrificed so much so that I could make this a reality. All of my love and deepest gratitude.

Published by The History Press
Charleston, SC 29403
www.historypress.net

Copyright © 2009 by Michael D. Coker
All rights reserved

First published 2009
Second printing 2011
Third printing 2013

ISBN 9781540219831

Library of Congress Cataloging-in-Publication Data

Coker, Mike.
The Battle of Port Royal / Michael D. Coker.
p. cm.
Includes bibliographical references.
ISBN 9781540219831
1. Port Royal (S.C.) Expedition, 1861. I. Title.
E472.7.C64 2009
975.7'99--dc22
2009043986

Notice: The information in this book is true and complete to the best of our knowledge. It is offered without guarantee on the part of the author or The History Press. The author and The History Press disclaim all liability in connection with the use of this book.

All rights reserved. No part of this book may be reproduced or transmitted in any form whatsoever without prior written permission from the publisher except in the case of brief quotations embodied in critical articles and reviews.

Contents

Acknowledgements   7

Chapter 1. They Had Come from Northern Shores Far Away   9
Chapter 2. Gallant Ships, Tempest-Toss'd   28
Chapter 3. Triumphant Still Their Course Southward Lay   35
Chapter 4. Those Shores So Serene   45
Chapter 5. Where Hilton Head and Low Bay Point Defied   49
Chapter 6. Iron Tempest in Incessant Blast   74
Chapter 7. Avenged Is Sumter's Humbled Flag at Last   106

Selected Bibliography   127

Acknowledgements

I wish to thank Laura All over at The History Press for countenancing delay after delay after delay after—you get the picture. She is an editor, and person, of the highest caliber. A lesser editor would have murdered me long ago (and would have been acquitted, I might add). I am also thanking, in advance, the rest of the hardworking staff at The History Press, from the line editors to the sales team. I know that "Team Clegg" (the Cleggers) and Amelia Lacey will do their utmost to sell this book, while Katie Parry will promote it to no end.

My family has been a tremendous source of support. My daughters, Jacqui and Eleanor, often got me through the day when nothing else could. My mother, Susie Wise, often babysat my youngest so I could spend a few hours in front of the computer. My mother-in-law, Jamie George, also provided moral support. Tom Ducker, my father-in-law, often encouraged me with kind words about my writing. Although he doesn't know it, my brother in-law, Matt Ducker, a fellow writer, is a model for my own writing. His commitment to the craft is nothing less than staggering.

I wish to thank the entire staff of the South Carolina Historical Society, especially Jane Aldrich and Mary Jo Fairchild. Archivist Karen Stokes went out of her way to locate hard-to-find material for me. Volunteer and naval historian Larry Grant answered my many questions patiently.

Grace Cordial, aptly named, at the Beaufort County Public Library, provided assistance. The folks at the Spindler Library in Michigan also took the time to mail a complete stranger some materials.

Acknowledgements

Dr. Stephen Wise, director of the Parris Island Marine Corps Museum and author of several excellent Civil War books, provided support and information. His years of research on the war in South Carolina are the groundwork for this book. I also drew heavily on the expertise of Dr. Lawrence Rowland, social historian bar none.

Inspiration came from many places, including Dr. Walter Edgar, one of the finest public historians South Carolina has ever produced. Dr. W. Eric Emerson at the South Carolina Department of Archives and History has encouraged my attempts at being a historian and remains something of a mentor to me.

During this project, I often read the work of master storyteller and South Carolinian Jonathan Hickman. Thanks for taking the graphic novel to new places. Speculative author Harry Turtledove must be credited with sparking my interest in the Civil War in the first place. I can still see the longhand of Mrs. Carol Cumming, my high school English teacher, in all of this. Although I was only in her class for one year, I am still running on the adrenaline for writing that she gave me.

To any I may have forgotten, please forgive my oversight and know that I do appreciate your assistance.

CHAPTER 1

THEY HAD COME FROM NORTHERN SHORES FAR AWAY

Shortly after five o'clock in the morning on Tuesday, October 29, 1861, the USS *Wabash* fired its signal gun. The noise reverberated over the still waters of Hampton Roads, echoing loudly off the stone walls of Fortress Monroe looming at the mouth of the harbor and sounding down into the deep holds of the ships moored nearby.

This was the call to arms for the largest fleet ever assembled by the United States. Never before had the nation concentrated this kind of destructive naval firepower in one place. Desperate times call for desperate measures; the country was unraveling, the "house was divided." Fort Sumter had fallen to the Confederates in April, and the Federal war effort had nearly dissolved after the disastrous Battle of Manassas back in July. News of the embarrassing defeat at Ball's Bluff six days earlier further dimmed hopes. The supposed blockade of Southern cities was something of an international joke. Winfield Scott's Anaconda Plan had failed to put crushing pressure on the rebellion; rather, it had delivered more of an ineffectual slap on the wrist. Coastal cities in the Confederacy continued their maritime traffic practically as they had before the war. Spirits had lifted at General Butler's success in the Cape Hatteras region. Now, the country was looking for a repeat of this combined operation on a much grander scale. This fleet—these men—were charged with nothing less than the task of changing the fortunes of the country.

Before the smoke from the signal gun had been carried away by the early morning breeze, the sailors started work. A stick had been jammed into the

The Battle of Port Royal

The Anaconda Plan

Library of Congress.

At the time of the Port Royal Expedition, American military thought had long been dictated by one man: General Winfield Scott. This venerable commander had served in every major conflict of the United States since the War of 1812. In 1841, he attained the title of general in chief of the United States Army. Hoping to cash in on his decades of military service, Scott ran for the office of president in 1851 but was defeated by Pierce. Scott continued on in his post under Pierce's administration and was still active in this role at the start of the Civil War.

Initially, Scott advocated a peaceful disunion with the Confederates, stating that they should let their "wayward sisters go in peace." When the Lincoln administration made clear its policy to put down the secession with force, Scott proposed another tactic. He advocated a massive maritime blockade of the Southern ports in conjunction with advances by land at key strategic points. This was to put interminable pressure on the seceding states. News of his proposal became public, and the press gave it the derisive name "Anaconda Plan," likening it to the serpent that kills its prey by constriction before devouring the corpse.

beehive. The ships were buzzing with the regular "jack-tars," novice landsmen, coal heavers, firemen and "powder monkeys" (small boys tasked with, among other things, the transportation of cartridges to the guns during a battle). Boatswains, those responsible for the upper deck, piped out their commands with uncharacteristic fervor. The decks were being hurriedly scrubbed, the brass polished, supplies stashed away, engines stoked and sails fixed. William John Abbot's *Blue Jackets of '61* captures the ensuing frenzy of activity:

> Soon from the black funnels of the steamers clouds of smoke began to pour and in the rigging of the sail frigates were crowds of nimble sailors. The commands "All ready! Let Fall!" rang sharply…Broad sheets of snowy canvas appeared where before were but ropes and spars.

They Had Come from Northern Shores Far Away

The plan was maligned; some even went so far as to claim treason. Scott was Virginia-born, and a distrustful few thought that his Anaconda Plan bore the hallmarks of a cop-out. It must have, they reasoned, emanated from the desk of someone who did not want to re-conquer his native state. The plan was never implemented as Scott had envisioned, but the principal idea was later seen in the blockade, which played an important role in the eventual Federal victory.

For nearly a month, this fleet—this decisive weapon of war—had sat idle and impatient behind Fortress Monroe. At the height of occupancy, the six-sided stone fort had cast its shadow over seventy ships and their complement of sailors, as well as their passengers—twelve thousand soldiers. Charles H. Davis, one of the naval officers, reflected on the appearance of the shipboard lamps: "This harbor of Hampton Roads looks like a great city, so numerous are the lights." Delay after delay—bureaucratic, logistical and flukes of nature—had kept them tethered in this corner of southeastern Virginia.

Perhaps no one would be gladder to be off the leash than the soldiers, many of whom had never before been aboard a ship. Upon hearing the signal gun, they swarmed up from below, getting underfoot of the busy sailors, and jostled for space along the rails of their transports. They had endured hours

The Blockade Is a Farce

The South was primarily agrarian at the time of the Civil War. The machines and factories needed to produce weapons and gunpowder were few in the Confederacy in 1861. To combat this deficiency, it was necessary to go abroad and import these much-needed resources. To impair the South's ability to bring in such items, a blockade of its coasts was ordered. To say that this was a grand scheme in 1861 would be an understatement. When Lincoln assumed the office of president, the United States Navy had just over forty ships in its service, and most of these were off in foreign waters. Yet Lincoln's April 1861 proclamation stated that "a competent force will be posted so as to prevent entrance and exit of vessels" at the ports in rebellion. This called for a navy that did not exist anywhere in the world at the time—one large enough to police over thirty-five hundred miles of coast.

However, the navy was up to the challenge. The shipyards began production, working around the clock, and purchasing agents snapped up merchant ships to convert them to military service. At the end of the first year of the war, the navy had a remarkable growth spurt; it could count on its rolls 260 ships. Construction was underway on another 100.

Despite these great gains, the blockade was ineffective in 1861. Ships were running back and forth from ports almost as before the war, leaving many on both sides to declare, "The blockade is a farce!"

of complicated drills, tramping off and on the ships at all hours of the day as they practiced their planned amphibious assault. For a week now they had been confined to the ship. The cramped conditions, bad food and questionable water made this tour of duty nearly unbearable.

Emmet Cole, a soldier in the Eighth Michigan stationed aboard the *Vanderbilt*, complained to his sister:

> *Here cramped up in a little hole just being enough to stick my head through the only place I can find where light shines from the top of the ship…I am getting tired of staying on this cussed old boat, all the soldiers are discontented here we don't get half so good fare here as we do on land. I can tell you what kind of fare we get here, it consists of what they call sailors biscuit and before I go any farter [sic] I must describe a biscuit, they are about four inches square and half an inch thick, you cannot taste a bit of salt in them, and they are as hard as the rock of ages. In addition to this we have once in a while a few potatoes boiled up the same as you boil them for the hogs and now and then a chunk of pork and coffee made of croton water that would puke the Devil himself.*

They Had Come from Northern Shores Far Away

Another soldier remarked that the salted beef issued them was practically unfit to eat—"the boys called it salt-horse." Needless to say, the soldiers were anxious to watch their ships take station, marking the beginning of their passage south and off these damn ships.

The sailors were equally as anxious to be back in their element, grateful to escape the prospect of a season of inactivity in port. A small group had taken part in the tiresome landing and boarding maneuvers, servicing the surfboats that were to carry the soldiers on the last leg of their objective. Under the watchful eyes of the fleet, the officers had practiced their joint operations on the small spit of land known as Old Point Comfort, just south of Fortress Monroe. The irony of performing such tiresome labor on a spot with such a name could not have escaped them.

Those old salts aboard the transports freighted with the soldiers were glad at the thought of shedding these irksome burdens. Space was tight enough aboard without these extra passengers. The men alone were bad enough, but for nearly two weeks their damnable horses had been penned in the holds of the ships. Below decks was a less pleasant place than ever. Then there were all of their carriages, tents, kits and crates and crates of provisions and ammunition. Once they dumped these nuisances and their clutter out of their holds, they could resume their normal duties. A statement by Commodore Samuel Du Pont, commander of the naval arm of this expedition, succinctly captures the attitude probably most in vogue with the veteran sailors: "Soldiers and marines are the most helpless people I ever saw."

Few in either branch of service were surprised that the signal had come on this day. The day before, twenty-five barges, packed with coal to fuel the steamers in the fleet and accompanied by several armed escorts, had departed. The night before, crates of hardtack, the staple of any campaign, had been hauled and stashed aboard in record numbers. These were clear indicators that the waiting was coming to a close.

A small flotilla of cutters struck out and rowed from ship to ship in the fleet before it pulled up anchor. The cutters were carrying officers with official dispatches—verbal commands—or had aboard personnel who had wandered ashore and struggled to get back on duty before being pronounced AWOL. Reporters from the *New York Tribune*, the *New York World* and the *New York Herald*, as well as a correspondent from the London-based *Star*, were embedded within the fleet. They pressed for details; at best, they got shrugs or informed opinion.

Speculation abounded as to their destination. Just where were they headed? South, into the lands of rebellion—that much was certain. Beyond that,

The Battle of Port Royal

Planning the Port Royal Expedition

On April 12, 1861, Gustavus Fox stood on the deck of the Baltic and watched the bombardment of the place he had come to save. His superiors had delayed and discussed for too long. Fort Sumter was being shelled by the Confederates, and there was nothing he could do about it. The supplies and men he had gathered—not to mention the hours he had spent planning—to reinforce the beleaguered troops of Major Anderson in the contested island fort were now worthless. The forty-year-old Massachusetts man had been in the navy since he was a teenager and knew that losing Sumter would be a strategic defeat and a stinging blow to the Federal morale.

Fox returned home with renewed determination not to let delays cost the navy another victory. His continued efforts gained him the position of chief clerk in the navy department in May 1861. He used his position to push an agenda of swift, aggressive campaigning. In August 1861, he was promoted to assistant secretary of the navy under Gideon Welles, a position that gave him more authority to push through his programs.

In the same month that Fox garnered his post as chief clerk, the Blockade Board was formed. This group, also called the Strategy Board and the Committee on Conference, was composed of some of the most distinguished naval theorists in the country: Samuel Du Pont (then a captain); Major John G. Barnard of the U.S. Engineer Corps; and Professor Alexander Bache, superintendent of the United States Coast Survey. Commander Charles Henry Davis acted as secretary. Fox would provide input into this group's deliberations.

Planning the Port Royal Expedition. *Author's collection.*

They Had Come from Northern Shores Far Away

Inside the old Smithsonian Institute in Washington, D.C., the men deliberated on how to implement the blockade to comply with Secretary Welles's directive to select points on the Confederate coast that could be used as coaling stations for the blockaders and staging areas for any possible army operations. Candidates for such a location inside South Carolina included Bull's Bay, St. Helena Sound and Port Royal Sound. The latter was the ultimate decision. The report of the Blockade Board summed up its decision, stating that Port Royal was the

> finest harbor south of Chesapeake Bay, which it resembles in capacity and extent. It is approached by three channels, the least of which has seventeen feet of water…Several of our screw frigates of the first class can pass the bar, and when the entrance is once made a whole navy can ride at anchor in the bay in uninterrupted health and security…The entrance is over two miles wide; there is fine anchorage under Bay Point; on the shore there is a number of roughhouses, the summer resort of planters. Water may be had at the Station Port Royal, Land's End…Near this point may be constructed a wharf for a coaling station above the mouth of the little creek…Port Royal is one of the wealthiest of the Sea Islands, and is devoted to the culture of sea-island cotton.

With the site chosen, Du Pont was appointed commander of the Southern Expedition, later called the Port Royal Expedition, in September 1861.

A Pennsylvanian visiting Port Royal in 1862, after the Union occupation, gives a wonderfully descriptive insight into the value of the area:

> It is not a matter of wonder that the first discoverers of this port and harbor were so struck with its magnificent proportions that they named it Port Royal; for in the eye of the mariner it is royal in every sense of the word. It is one of the finest harbors in the world, and the best on the Southern Atlantic coast. The bar has a depth of water to float the largest vessel; while inside there opens a broad estuary, with capacity to contain the navies of the world, with a good anchorage.

suspects. Not even the commanders of the ships knew their destination. Spies and over-eager newspapermen were all too keen to broadcast their plans, alerting their adversary, so their ultimate destination was a tightly guarded secret. In fact, a rumor spread that a Federal officer had absconded with the signal book of the *Dawn*, of the Potomac squadron, with designs to pass on the secret codes to the Confederates. The truth of this rumor had yet to be verified, but it was taken seriously enough at this critical juncture. The day before, Samuel Du Pont had gotten the message to alter the numbers in his ships' signal books, rendering the theft of the *Dawn*'s book harmless. Du Pont wanted to maintain the element of surprise as long as possible. Captains of the ships were given a sealed envelope with strict instructions to break the wax seal only when at sea or in dire circumstances, such as separation.

Wherever they were headed didn't really matter; the fact that they were headed somewhere was reason enough for celebration. By 5:30 a.m., the nautical behemoth had begun to move. Boisterous cheers erupted from the men massed along the railings. Musicians from the ranks grabbed their instruments, formed bands and began to play spritely military airs.

Inside Fortress Monroe, Major General John E. Wool, commander of the Department of Virginia, breathed a sigh of relief. Fortress Monroe had played host to these visitors for too long, in Wool's opinion, doling out supplies, water and ammunition as requested. The ravenous expedition had even begun eyeing his artillerymen, wanting to appropriate them from Monroe and into its ranks. In a testy letter to the secretary of war, Simon Cameron, Wool complained of these many impositions and offered his opinion on the whole affair: "I will venture to assert that a worse-managed expedition could not well be contrived."

This was clearly not the popular sentiment of the morning. Wool's men had turned out to watch from the walls and cheer on their brethren. The residents of the area had turned out, too, drawn out of their homes by the noise. They gathered to shout their approval from the banks.

Brigadier General Egbert Viele, one of the army officers aboard, recalled that "both shores of the magnificent harbor were lined with spectators." He also remembered that not all wished them well. This section of Virginia was near the frontline. The Confederates still controlled the south bank of the James River, one of several of the rivers flowing out from Hampton Roads. A seacoast battery, out of range of the fleet's guns, had been placed at Sewell's Point, opposite Fortress Monroe. "From one side came blessings, from the other curses—for those serene waters constituted the dividing line between the two sections of the country arrayed in deadly warfare."

They Had Come from Northern Shores Far Away

Samuel Du Pont

Samuel Francis Du Pont—"Frank" to his friends and family—was fifty-eight years old at the time of the Port Royal Expedition. At the young age of twelve, he began his naval career as a midshipman. He served onboard a variety of ships for the next several decades, pursuing his education in between domestic and international tours. In 1826, he married Sophie Du Pont, a first cousin (a practice not uncommon in the nineteenth century) and the daughter of his uncle who had founded the famous powder works. Sophie's lingering illness often caused Du Pont to refuse assignments too far abroad.

In 1845, Du Pont, because of his experience, was chosen as one of the commanders to select the site and establish the curriculum of the prestigious naval academy at Annapolis. The Mexican War took Du Pont away from Sophie; he served in Mexican and Californian waters during that conflict.

After that war, Du Pont spent the next decade on land, working as a logistical and technical reformer of his beloved service. In 1857, he was invited to join the Naval Academy and

Library of Congress.

Lighthouse Board, a prestigious think tank on coastal navigation, cementing his reputation as an officer of the highest caliber. The next year, he took an assignment aboard the new steam frigate the Minnesota, *touring in the Far East and visiting such ports of call as Japan, Hong Kong and India. By 1860, he was back in the United States, serving as commandant of the Philadelphia Navy Yard. In June 1861, Du Pont's reputation garnered him a spot on the Blockade Board, which led to his appointment as head of the South Atlantic Blockading Squadron in September. Skillful execution of these duties made him the choice to head up the Port Royal Expedition.*

The success at Port Royal added more luster to Du Pont's rising star. Several poems and songs were written in his honor, and his name and face were splashed all over the newspapers. Congress voted him an official in appreciation of his efforts at Port Royal.

This worship experienced a backlash in 1863. Du Pont was head of a much-publicized ironclad fleet attack against the Charleston defenses. The ironclads were soundly defeated by the Confederates. Although supported by his subordinates, Du Pont became a scapegoat for this humiliating defeat. At his request, he stepped down from command and bitterly retired from active military service until 1865. At the coaxing of another naval officer, Du Pont had agreed to serve on a military board. Unfortunately, he died on June 23, 1865, before he could begin service. A large monument in his honor sits in Du Pont Circle in Washington, D.C.

General Isaac Ingalls Stevens, one of the army officers, wrote:

Thus the mighty armada steadily plowed its way out to sea, with flags waving and bands playing, a glorious and awe-inspiring sight; while the troops, exhilarated by the novel and stirring scene and the excitement of sailing to an unknown destination, their hearts swelling with the hope and determination of soon dealing the rebel lion a mighty and perhaps fatal blow, cheered and cheered again until they could cheer no more.

In three elegant lines, the fleet passed through Hampton Roads, cut across the Chesapeake and headed out into the Atlantic. Northern newspapers had assigned it the moniker the "Great Southern Expedition," while some Southerners referred to it as the "Lincoln Fleet." It was a motley assortment. Viele noted, "The exigencies of the case had caused the drafting into the service of every description of craft-ocean steamers, coasters, sailing vessels, ferry boats, river steamers." Four of the fighting vessels were new—part of the ninety-day gunboat plan, meaning that just over three months earlier the timbers of these ships had still been growing in the forests. Like many of the men aboard, they were raw, unseasoned.

BLUEJACKETS AND CONTRABANDS

Some of the soldiers and sailors had more personal reasons to be uncomfortable. One thousand African American men—slaves who had fled bondage to come into the safety of Fortress Monroe—had been organized and placed with the fleet. The United States was not yet ready to grant these men their freedom or make them soldiers. Nor was the United States willing to take a stance on slavery as an institution. Slaves from states not in rebellion were to be refused entrance into Fort Monroe; only slaves from the seceding states were to be granted sanctuary. These men were designated "contrabands"—living war material seized from the enemy—and were to aid in the backbreaking labor of setting up a permanent camp once the fleet completed its objective.

Abolitionists were a minority in the Federal war effort, so the very presence of these men caused discomfort in the fleet. The career sailors were probably the ones least impacted by their presence. The United States Navy was ahead of the rest of the country in one respect. Even before the Civil War, the navy had recruited able-bodied seamen regardless of race and promoted worthy individuals through the lower ranks. There were free men of color among the sailors wearing the Union blue—the "bluejackets"—who took part in this October expedition. How would they fare if their ship was boarded and they were captured, many wondered? Would they be treated as prisoners of war or dealt with more harshly because of the color of their skin? The contrabands faced a similar dilemma, but few questioned their fortunes should this excursion fail and their former masters gain possession of them again. If not executed, contrabands would quickly revert back to slaves.

CONTRABANDS ENTERING A CAMP WITHIN THE UNION LINES.

Author's collection.

The Battle of Port Royal

> *Dr. Lisa King, in her landmark essay "They Called Us Bluejackets," gives insight into the life of one of these contrabands, William H. Fitzhugh, who paid the ultimate sacrifice. Fitzhugh had joined the navy and served as a first-class boy onboard the USS* Pawnee.
>
> An enemy shell struck the ship and exploded at the waterline killing ordinary seaman John Kelly instantly. Splinters from the impact shattered Fitzhugh's right leg. In an effort to save him, the surgeon amputated his leg, but Fitzhugh died later that evening probably never knowing of the Union victory that he participated in that day. He was buried with full military honors at Bay Point the next day with the other seven men killed in battle. William Fitzhugh was a contraband of war, that is, a recently, self-emancipated slave who found his way to the Union line in Virginia and enlisted in the Navy. Fitzhugh may be the first black casualty for the South Atlantic Blockading Squadron but he was in no way unique in his naval service.

The flagship was the USS *Wabash*, the forty-gun veteran that had seen service in the Mediterranean just a few years earlier. From its deck, the signal gun that had touched off the exodus had been fired. Now, attention was focused on its flags. In the age before radio, ships acting in concert communicated with one another through the use of signal flags. Harbor pilots and officers knew the most common signals on sight, and the more complicated could be looked up in the signal book. Those closest to the *Wabash* could see the signals and relayed the commands back to those out of visual contact. Mrs. Du Pont had once asked her husband about the responsibilities of a flagship. In response, he told her:

> *The flagship governs a great deal: follow motions without or with signals is a general order. The going to dinner is to ensure the crews their meals at regular times—and to call back boats, etc., and to keep boats to be given for the convenience of people and thus disturbing the men, who have so few comforts compared with us.*

In his memoirs, Davis wrote of the slow beginning of the fleet: "It took some time…to get under way, especially as they were to move in an established order, which brought them all in point of speed, to a level with the dullest. It was well we started early." It had taken nearly six hours to get past Cape Henry, a point

They Had Come from Northern Shores Far Away

> ### USS *Wabash*
>
> *The first ship to bear the designation USS* Wabash *was built at the Philadelphia Navy Yard in 1855 and commissioned in 1856. The* Pennsylvanian *newspaper was on hand for its launch: "The beauty of the hull, and its apparent strength was the subject of general remark." The finished craft was a three-masted steam screw frigate measuring an impressive 301 feet long (an "extreme length" in 1856) and 51 feet abeam. Forty heavy guns were placed over the vessel, making it a fearsome engine of war.*
>
> *During its inaugural run, the* Wabash *transported then President Franklin Pierce from Portsmouth to Annapolis. In 1856, it became flagship of Commodore Hiram Paulding's Home Squadron and then served abroad in the Mediterranean. The* Wabash *was called home at the outbreak of the Civil War and became the flagship of the South Atlantic Blockading Squadron. The ship and its crew were present in the early days of the blockade of Charleston, participated in the capture of the Cape Hatteras area and led the Port Royal Expedition. After the fall of Hilton Head, the ship continued its duty as a blockader and flagship. Its last major campaign was the Fort Fisher campaign in late 1864 and early 1865. The ship was deactivated later that year but returned to flagship status in the Mediterranean in the 1870s. From 1876 to 1912, the* Wabash *performed a very different duty: it served as a receiving ship in the Boston Navy Yard. In 1912, the ship that had played such an important role in the Civil War was burned in order to make retrieval of its metal parts easier.*

of roughly twenty miles. Once south of this location, the *Wabash* gave the order to form a double-echelon line, or a V-shaped formation.

The *Wabash* took the point, and the other ships were to stretch out in parallel wings, all pointed in a common direction. Some of the smaller, swifter boats, like the *Atlantic*, operated on the flanks of the columns, serving as nautical shepherds for the wayward, drifting fleet member. Not all of the ship commanders were experienced hands; completion of this maneuver took some time to accomplish. The first casualty of the expedition occurred during this shuffling. The gunboat *Unadilla*, launched the previous month, became disabled and had to be towed by another ship. The *Unadilla* would not be the only ship towed—the sailing ships that lacked steam engines, and the smaller or older craft that were unable to keep pace, were hitched to the more powerful steamers.

The fleet traveled in this fashion, stretched out over six square miles of ocean, for the next thirty-six hours. During an uneventful period, Davis found time to stare out from the deck of the *Wabash* and pen his thoughts on sailing amidst so many other ships:

The Battle of Port Royal

> *The appearance of the fleet at night was as impressive as it was uncommon. I have...never known what it was to be in company with more than two ships at a time, and that seldom. A light at night in the open sea has rather been regarded as an object of apprehension, particularly if the night was dark, because before finding out the direction in which the stranger was standing, there was a fear of running foul of him. But now, at night, the sea is covered with lights at every point of the horizon, on both sides and astern. Ahead there are none, because this ship is the centre of the leading line. But viewing the scene from the quarterdeck, the absence of lights in the ships head is not felt. Steamers carry several lights each, of which one on the port side is red and that on the starboard side is green. Variety was not or is not wanting, therefore to add to the glitter and effect of the show. We seem to be in the midst of a populous community, and yet we do not lose the feeling of being at sea. I am more than charmed with the sight.*

Davis concludes this entry by reflecting that this is what the great fleets in times past must have looked like, and he felt sympathy for those sailors of olden times because they lacked the advantage of steam engines. It was not long before Davis found himself regretting his pride.

Along the way, the *Atlantic* found time to practice its land assault. Flat-bottom boats called lighters were lowered over the side of the transport, loaded with soldiers carrying their equipment. The lighters were rowed out to a stretch of barren, sandy Virginia beach, technically the territory of their foes. As they had done in Hampton Roads, they disembarked from the boats, waded ashore and moved into battle formation. It was hoped that these techniques would allow them to mass in great number and storm the works at Hilton Head.

On Wednesday, October 30, Lieutenant Henry H. Ayer of the *Atlantic* penned a letter describing their progress: "We are about 40 miles from land...It is getting rough, and the small gunboats are beginning to pitch and roll badly." This bad weather wreaked havoc on the formation, forcing some of the smaller ships to hug the coast. Later in the day, a ferryboat traveling with the fleet hoisted "ensign union down," a signal of distress. The *Augusta* pulled back to investigate, and by the time it returned to its place in line, Du Pont had noted that the ferryboat that had signaled was no longer in sight, nor were a number of other ferryboats and tugs. He surmised that the foul weather had forced the less seaworthy craft back to Hampton Roads. He reflected on this unforeseen setback in his journal:

> *I am sorry at this first contretemps—but will dispatch a steamer after them the moment we get down. These small craft have given us much trouble in their organization—to get them down was a lottery at best.*

They Had Come from Northern Shores Far Away

THE MISSING MR. BOUTELLE

A few days before the departure of the expedition, Du Pont wrote a letter to his wife, Sophie, filling her in on the latest news from Hampton Roads. In that October 24 missive, he also listed several problems that had arisen that might hamper the expedition but dismissed them with a falsely cavalier attitude: "These things do not trouble but the absence of Boutelle does." In the same letter, he explains that "Mr. Boutelle, without whom it seems impossible to attempt Port Royal, is not here."

Who was this man upon whom so much depended but whose name is seldom connected with the Port Royal Expedition? Charles O. Boutelle was in his late forties in 1861 and had worked for six years as a coast survey assistant, making hydrographic surveys in the Port Royal area. Du Pont knew the value of such information: "He Knows every foot of ground around Port Royal, made the triangulation and carried the 'Brooklyn' in eighteen months ago." There was doubt whether the juggernaut, the Wabash, *would be able to get into the harbor, concern that is reflected in Du Pont's statement: "He could tell us with recent local knowledge if the 'Wabash' can get in." Boutelle had even resided in nearby Beaufort, South Carolina, while surveying and had become part of that community. In short, he had vital information that Du Pont desperately needed.*

Du Pont had made arrangements to appropriate Boutelle earlier and have him on hand. Now, in the final days of the expedition, this critical component was nowhere to be found. He was to have come into Hampton Roads by rail but instead was coming from New York by ship. Waiting for his arrival could cause a fatal delay to the expedition.

On October 26, after two more wearying days overseeing details, Du Pont wrote to Sophie again, remarking:

> Tired and my eyes having reached the stopping point after good many letters necessary to write…I threw myself on a sofa with a cigar and thought of you…worried by only one event, the nonappearance of Mr. Boutelle. But I did not fret nor repine; indeed the feeling that any one man was indispensable to us would be mortifying so I resigned myself.

Du Pont was awoken by shipboard racket "earlier than my want" but had a pleasant surprise. As he dressed, he heard a strange voice addressing one of his subordinates outside his cabin. He "instinctively concluded it was Mr. Boutelle, and so it proved so." The fleet commander had not been the only one aware of the need for Boutelle. Charles Henry Davis, one of Du Pont's staff, was thrilled when this gentleman finally appeared:

The Battle of Port Royal

> He was very welcome; nothing could have supplied the loss of his knowledge of the ground. He made the triangulation, the groundwork of the survey, of the whole coast of South Carolina, and he possesses a taste for topographical details, and a facility of observing, and so to speak, of interpreting them, which are truly wonderful.

Logistical error had prevented Boutelle from arriving sooner. He arrived aboard the Vixen *and immediately headed for the flagship. "The generals are now in the forward cabin with him going over great topographical maps," Davis noted, recalling the activity onboard the* Wabash *after Boutelle's arrival.*

> The first thing after breakfast was to send for the other generals and have another council of war…The generals talked…with Mr. Boutelle, while Du Pont and I wrote without cessation, preparing the final orders…Mr. Boutelle answered all their questions…he satisfied me upon the only point about which I felt anxious; that is, the easy and certain entrance of this ship into that place *[Port Royal]*.

Great use was made of Boutelle's specialized knowledge during the planning sessions. During the battle, he served as captain of the Vixen. *General T.W. Sherman made special mention of him in his after-action report: "It is my duty to report the valuable services of Mr. Boutelle…His services are invaluable to the Army as well as to the Navy." After the occupation of the Hilton Head area, Boutelle's knowledge of the region was frequently consulted. However, this earned him the lasting enmity of his former Southern neighbors.*

He commented on the oversight of his subordinates at not having these vessels of dubious quality towed in the first place but vowed, "I am not going to fret for this small matter, provided the people on board are safe."

Later that night, the weather altered again. Du Pont wrote:

> We have a gale from the southwest; the weather is clear, however…It retards much our progress; we are to pass close the shoals off Hatteras, to avoid the Gulf Stream which would carry us to the northeast.

In the early morning hours of the thirty-first, the fleet rounded Cape Hatteras, giving a berth of six miles to the shoals of that region. During this

They Had Come from Northern Shores Far Away

procedure, it experienced another mishap: two of the transports struck the shoal. Aboard the *Wabash*, Officer John S. Barnes wrote that it was about 2:30 a.m. when they received the dreaded "ship ashore" signal from one of the vessels cruising near the coast. Had one of their own been battered to pieces on the shoal? Ten rockets flared up from the deck of another vessel in distress. Barnes noted:

> *The greatest anxiety prevailed. The sea ran so high that no ship fairly on the shoals could possibly get off nor could any help be extended...A great disaster seemed certain....Nothing could be done and nothing was done. We kept on our way, hoping for the best.*

Du Pont was far less emotional—he only barely described this scene and noted that he had decided not to trouble the flagship. He trusted that the gunboats he had placed on the flank of the column closest to the coast would attend to the crisis. When it had grown light enough to make a visual survey of the fleet, Du Pont's calm was shaken. The fleet had lost more ships! Again, Barnes leaves a more personal recollection: "Daylight revealed thirty-one vessels of our fleet in sight, twenty had disappeared in one night." To gather intelligence on the events of the previous night, Du Pont telegraphed the *Florida*, which was in a position to have witnessed the evening's events, to come within hailing distance.

Author's collection.

The Battle of Port Royal

> ## Extract of Du Pont's Letter to Assistant Secretary Fox upon Leaving Hampton Roads
>
> *My Dear Sir,*
>
> *Please inform Mr. Welles that we are off...Twenty-eight days ago this expedition, though long meditated...had no form or substance...The ships in my squadron are in as high condition as I can expect...We have considerable power to carry on an offensive warfare; that of endurance against forts is not commensurate. But in so righteous a cause as ours, and against so wicked a rebellion, we must overcome all difficulties.*

Captain Goldsborough relayed the information that he had learned from another gunboat: it had been the *Illinois* that had sent up the rockets. The *Illinois* was in "the breakers "(a nautical term meaning that the ship had gotten mired in the zone where waves approaching the coastline commenced breaking apart) but was still very much afloat. Goldsborough also reported that several of the missing steamers had also got into the breakers, but all were steering back out to sea. Du Pont was understandably relieved after this conference. His concern must have been further alleviated by a second report from the *Belvidere*. This ship approached the *Wabash* to impart the news that it had spotted several of the missing ships safely at anchor in Hatteras.

In a letter penned the next day, Du Pont expressed his frustration at this incident:

> *We doubled Cape Hatteras last night, a little too close, not for our safety, with our care and attention to such things, but too close for careless, stupid skippers, or second- and third-class merchant captains.*

Conditions seemed to improve the rest of the day; Du Pont referred to the remainder of that last day in October as "smooth sea." A soldier in the Third New Hampshire concurred: "The wind had gone down, and it was a perfect calm, except a long swell on the sea." As he was writing years after the war, safe in his home, he was privy to insight that Du Pont, who wrote that same day, lacked. The soldier added ominously, "This proved to be the calm preceding a storm."

They Had Come from Northern Shores Far Away

The weather soured on November 1 after the fleet had rounded the cape. Rain slashed downward, the wind rose and the sky darkened, gradually shutting out the light. The temperature spiked, making below decks, especially near the engines, a disagreeable place. Even the most clueless soldiers could surmise that a gale was upon them. The *Isaac Smith* signaled its distress and then fell off in the "trough of the sea." Du Pont ordered the reliable *Florida* and the *Atlantic* to its assistance. As the *Wabash* plowed ahead, it signaled that all craft not already doing so should "heave to." According to Du Pont, "That is turning their bows or prows towards the wind and sea, to ride over more easily and prevent the rolling motion."

At 2:30 p.m., the *Wabash* sent out the order to disregard the previously prescribed order of sailing, freeing the captains to do what they thought was best to survive the night ahead. Du Pont hoped this would be enough.

CHAPTER 2

Gallant Ships, Tempest-Toss'd

The storm swept over the fleet with a scolding fury, hurling wind, rain, thunder, lightning and a seemingly endless succession of waves against the motley assortment of Federal ships. Isolated, swept apart by the vicious currents, the sailors and the soldiers aboard—those who were not too seasick to stand—fought to keep their battered ships afloat. Darkness surrounded them, their lanterns fragile pinpricks of luminescence. Light of a more surreal fashion was provided by the phosphorescent glow of animalcule, the luminous sea creatures dredged up from the depths that swirled within the sheet of foam coating the sea.

Many of those trapped aboard these vessels must have been struck by the black humor of this situation. The largest, most powerful naval force ever assembled by the United States was in danger of being obliterated, without ever having fired a shot in battle.

According to one chronicler of this expedition, some of the sailors recalled General Butler's nautical invasion of this area earlier in the year. While Butler's foray had yielded some successes, foul weather had hampered operations, spreading superstition through the ranks: "They conceived Hatteras to be tenanted by an evil spirit, determined to prevent the invasion of Confederate territory." Should destruction be their fate, their former countrymen, now foreigners living in the newly minted Confederate States of America, would view their demise not as the work of an evil spirit but as the design of a kind and just God. For years afterward, innumerable Southern ministers would declare from their Sunday pulpits that this tempest was a heaven-sent miracle.

Gallant Ships, Tempest-Toss'd

The Great Storm scatters the expedition. *Author's collection.*

Lieutenant Daniel Ammen, aboard the *Seneca*, was skilled enough to know that this particular storm was not divinely or sulfurously sparked. This was simply the angry temperament, the talon reach, of the cape, dubbed the "Graveyard of the Atlantic" for good reason. At forty-one years of age, Ammen had already spent two and a half decades in the navy. His lengthy service had taken him through the waters of the West Indies, the Mediterranean, East India and Brazil. He had logged many months of domestic service as well, formerly stationed for a period on the West Coast of the United States. Ammen was no stranger to the East Coast, however; his days of coastal surveying had brought him through Cape Hatteras before. From atop lighthouses, he had studied the geography of this petulant headland. There were few nights when lightning did not hang menacingly overhead.

For the rest of the night, Ammen hunkered under the protective weather bulwark of his ship, close to the wheel. His experience, and the attention of his crew, would bring the *Seneca* through the night, rattled but intact. There were other ships in the fleet that had equally skilled crews and commanders, yet fate had woven them a different design.

A soldier known only as D.E. left the following account of the *Atlantic*'s struggle:

> The old Atlantic, which was considered the most staunch craft of the fleet, was tossed like an egg shell. The barrels of pork and beef in the hold were thrown from side to side with such force that it really seemed we should be stove. During the day, the scene was a grand one. The waves ran mountains

GENERAL THOMAS WEST SHERMAN

Library of Congress.

While this Federal officer shared the surname of one of the Civil War's most iconic figures—General William T. Sherman—the two were not related. This Sherman was born in Rhode Island in 1813. His family was of modest means and reputation, which made gaining an appointment to West Point, the nation's premier military school, no easy task. Nonetheless, he successfully entered and graduated from the school. His first post took him into the middle of the war that was raging between the Unites States and the Seminole Indians in Florida (known as the Second Seminole War). His two years in the Florida wilds likely served him well during his next tour of duty against the Cherokee nation in 1838. During the Mexican War, Sherman occupied the office of quartermaster with the rank of captain. His valor at the Battle of Buena Vista earned him the rank of brevet major. For the next few decades, he saw duty on the rugged western frontier.

The Civil War returned him back east to Maryland, where he oversaw an artillery company and later became a brigadier general of volunteers. Sherman was stationed aboard the flagship Wabash, *giving Du Pont a chance to evaluate him. Du Pont noted, "He is more able a general than I thought; instead of being a mere sabreur, he studies maps, has informed himself well of his work. I think we shall work harmoniously."*

In 1862, Sherman was transferred back into the Gulf area and lost a leg leading an assault on Port Hudson. This wound limited his ability to be in a combat zone, and he was placed in a reserve post. On March 13, his bravery at the Battle of Port Hudson was officially recognized; he was appointed brevet major general. He retired from the military in 1870, leaving behind an impressive thirty-four-year record. Sherman returned home to his native Rhode Island and passed away in 1879.

high. Sometimes, when upon a high wave we could see several of the smaller crafts struggling for life with the invisible foe, with signals of distress flying that could not be answered—as no vessel could safely approach another in such a storm, lest, both go to the bottom. This scene would be suddenly cut off by our noble steamer sinking below everything visible, and the walls of *the sea upon either side would seem ready to fall inward and engulf us; and again, as suddenly, we would be raised to a point overlooking the sad sight before mentioned. We were thus situated for two days and three nights, with death staring us in the face we knew He was working fearfully near us.*

Placed on the *Bienville*, a reporter from the *New York World* lived to tell of his similar experience:

One moment we were on top of a wave, and could distinguish the position of the vessels in the fleet by the multitude of signal lights that were swung in the rigging, and the next instant we were down in the trough of the sea, with the avalanche of waters rearing its giant walls each side of our noble craft…the rain poured down in torrents as the night closed in, and the darkness became intense, being relieved only by the lightning that broke in sheets of flame from the heavens, almost blinding our eyes and rendering the darkness more intense.

John Rodgers

There were two Rodgerses serving aboard the Wabash *with Du Pont in 1861—cousins C.R.P. Rodgers and John Rodgers. One biographer has referred to John Rodgers as the "Quintessential Nineteenth-Century Naval Officer." He came by it honestly. He was the son of a naval commodore and shared his name. His career path seemed to be already laid out for him.*

At the age of sixteen, he received an appointment as midshipman in the navy. He served the far-flung Mediterranean Squadron. In 1834, he returned stateside, took a leave of absence and attended the University of Virginia. In 1839, he was stationed among the small naval contingent that participated in the Second Seminole War. His service in that theater earned him a long-awaited promotion to lieutenant.

In 1842, Rodgers was subject to a hearing for cruel treatment of the men under his command. While in Florida, he had ordered some drunken subordinates lashed in excesses of thirty times apiece. One of the sailors had died soon afterward, and one of the crewmen blamed Rodgers.

Rodgers was cleared of any wrongdoing and continued his naval career. In the 1850s, he was in command of the North Pacific Exploring and Surveying Expedition. At the time of secession, Rodgers was back in the United States, in Washington, D.C., where he met and wed Ann Elizabeth Hodge. He took part in the Federal evacuation of the Norfolk Navy Yard. In an attempt to deprive the Confederates use of the facilities, he tried to blow up the navy yard. This attempt failed, and Rodgers was captured and held for a short period of time by irate Confederates.

Upon his release, he was transferred to Cincinnati with instructions to help create a flotilla of riverboats. Four eventful months later he returned to D.C. He became involved with Du Pont and took a post on the Wabash *in time to participate in the Port Royal Expedition. Du Pont wrote to his wife that Rodgers was "a peculiar man but of great ability in various ways."*

Rodgers stayed with the South Atlantic Squadron after the conclusion of the Port Royal Expedition. In July 1862, he was promoted to the rank of captain and transferred to the monitor Weehawken. *He participated in the ill-fated ironclad attack on Charleston in 1863 that cost Du Pont his command. Rodgers continued in service on the monitor and was instrumental in capturing the Confederate ram* Atlanta. *This capture won him the thanks of Congress, similar to the one Du Pont had earned for Port Royal, and promotion to the position of commodore, with the rank of rear admiral obtained postwar. He died in 1882 while acting as superintendent of the United States Naval Observatory.*

A soldier of the Sixth Connecticut wrote:

> *For several hours the prospect of seeing anything but a broken wreck and a watery grave, were exceedingly dubious. Wave after wave poured over us. The hatches were fastened and everything on deck was lashed tight to prevent being washed away. The red glare of the lightning, with the terrific peals of thunder, made the scene awfully grand.*

Onboard the *Wabash*, Du Pont recalled:

> *We closed ports and bailed bucket after bucket…During the night it was the same old story—fetching sway of furniture, rolling of glasses and bottles about the sideboard, rolling of sofas. So hot and close below, blowing great guns above with torrents of rain. In spite of the engines the ship drifting fast ashore, great many lights still in sight from the ships—collision occupying our minds*

Gallant Ships, Tempest-Toss'd

some, but mine more on the small fry, thinking if this great leviathan could be made to twist, roll, and writhe as she did, what must those tiny vessels in comparison be doing?

Charles H. Davis gives a harrowing account of the storm:

By dark our number was sadly reduced, and about ten o' clock, when the storm raged the loudest, we entertained the most anxious fears for the safety of one or two of the weakest and less stanch of our little companions, and to these fears was added the dread of collision. On board this great ship, such an accident was little alarming on our account. But if we had fallen on board one of the transports she must inevitably have gone to the bottom. The violence of the wind, the height of the sea, the storm of rain...made it impossible to avoid collision, or to render assistance after it occurred.

In his 1885 regimental history of the Forty-Eighth New York, Abraham J. Palmer noted:

The storm was as grand as it was terrible, and it scattered that noble fleet of vessels to the winds. It has often been compared to the tempest which destroyed the Spanish Armada three centuries before...The writer has twice crossed the

Signaling the flagship *Wabash*. Author's collection.

ocean, and five times since passed Hatteras, but never has witnessed so terrible a storm at sea.

As soon as possible the next morning, Du Pont and Davis were topside on the *Wabash*, anxiously surveying the choppy waters in all directions with hand-held spyglasses. Davis wrote that Saturday, November 2,

opened with the usual appearance of a storm at sea—an angry sky, rain, wind, and a general appearance of discomfort on board and of desolation on the dreary waste of waters; wet decks, darkness below and great motion.

Over fifty ships had left Hampton Roads. In the wake of the storm, only one other sail was visible on the horizon. This desolation struck Davis: "The most impressive feature of the scene was the solitude. We had sailed from port with a fleet...the ocean was alive with our numbers; and now we were scattered in a storm."

Out of sight of Du Pont and Davis floated another survivor, the steamer *Matanzas*. From its deck, Private Abraham Palmer surveyed the scene, asking the same questions that were plaguing the officers on the *Wabash*:

On the morning, when the storm had subsided...not a sail was in sight. Had they gone down in the sea? Were they scattered so far apart that no one of the ships was in sight of another? What had become of the weaker and less seaworthy vessels?

CHAPTER 3

TRIUMPHANT STILL THEIR COURSE SOUTHWARD LAY

While waiting for some sign of the other ships, the crew inspected the *Wabash* for damage. It had endured remarkably well, suffering only minor scratches. Mercifully, the storm had chosen not to use the flagship as a weapon; the big ship was not driven onto another smaller member of the fleet. "Thank God we escaped that horror," Davis remarked. Du Pont had forgotten to close the port on his side, and six inches of water flooded his cabin, ruining carpets but little else. The mainmast would have to be restrengthened, but the holes were plugged for the time being. Other than these small considerations, the flagship was in the shape it had been in when it left Hampton Roads.

As the day wore on, the mood aboard the *Wabash* lifted. Several ships had started to straggle in. Some brought news of others still far from view. Davis recollected, "Of our companions only eight could be discerned with difficulty and rarely, as the rain and heavy mist abated and cleared away at short and infrequent intervals." Earlier in the voyage, Davis had marveled at the might of their numbers and extolled their advanced technology. It seemed hubris to him now: "If I experienced any of the puffing-up of the spirit…the changes brought by Friday…was suited to rebuke it…We passed a grave and thoughtful day."

A small riverboat christened the *Mayflower* came into view of the *Wabash*. The "ensign union down" signal flew from its masts. The boat had not been designed for ocean travel, and although it had survived the night, it was crippled. Again, Davis noted, "It was evident from her conduct that she was abandoned to despair. She was drifting like a log towards the Gulf Stream, where she must have foundered, in her helpless condition, unless picked up." The sheer size of the *Wabash* worked against it in this case; maneuvering round to aid such a frail vessel in a still heavy sea was impossible. Captain Eldridge of the newly reappeared *Atlantic* came to the rescue. A hawser, a thick coil of ropes, was extended to the *Mayflower*, and the disabled point became another tow.

Soon the casualties of the storm became apparent. The transport *Peerless* was claimed by the waves, its crew brought off safely by the efforts of Captain Gordon and the *Mohican*. The 1861 edition of the *National History of the War for the Union, Civil, Military and Naval Founded on Official and Other Authentic Documents* provided a more thorough account of this incident:

> *The* Peerless, *a small steamer formerly employed on Lake Ontario, between Winston and Toronto, laden with beef cattle, also fell a victim to the gale. She gave signals of distress when the* Star of the South *came up and in the tumult of the storm unhappily ran into her quarter. She was so much injured by the collision, that though the cattle, eighty-seven in number, were thrown overboard to lighten her, she was unable further to struggle with the waves. The gunboat* Mohican, *Commander Gordon, came to her aid, and took off all on board, twenty-six in number. The captain was the last to leave the fast sinking vessel. He quietly launched his life-boat, placed his trunk in it and reached his deliverer in perfect safety.*

The *Isaac Smith* still sailed but had to offer the ocean a very expensive sacrifice—all but one of its guns had been cast overboard to stay afloat. The *Osceola*, carrying in its hold another cargo of live cattle to be slaughtered for beef, was wrecked on North Island off Winyah Bay near Georgetown, South Carolina. Confederates rounded up twenty dazed survivors of the wreck and made prisoners of war of them. The *Union*, under the command of Captain Sawin, sank offshore of Beaufort, North Carolina, spoiling a cargo of gunpowder. Seventy-three of its crew and passengers were also made POWs. The *Winfield Scott*, the steamer named in honor of the general in chief, had nearly avoided destruction after wrecking during the storm. The *National History of the War* offers the following gripping account:

> *The* Winfield Scott, *government transport, a new iron steamer, barely escaped destruction. She had on board five hundred men of the*

Triumphant Still Their Course Southward Lay

50th Pennsylvania regiment, whose efficient conduct assisted greatly in the preservation of the ship. She had been laboring fearfully all Friday afternoon and night, when the discovery was made about one A.M. that the after hold contained five feet of water. An examination showed an extensive leak around the rudder-head, and, what was still more alarming, that the woodwork of the upper part of the vessel, at its uniting point with the iron hull, on the whole of the starboard side, abaft the wheel, yawed open at every lurch, affording an entrance for immense volumes of water. The Captain immediately ordered the ship to be lightened, by throwing overboard her cargo, and two rifled cannon, which constituted his armament. This was commenced, and the after hold soon afterwards was emptied of the immense quantities of provisions, tents and camp equipage which it contained. The soldiers worked energetically with the crew in baling, and their efforts were vastly more arduous in consequence of the choking of the vessel's steam pump by the rubbish in the hold. This labor was persistently kept up during the whole night, but all they could do only sufficed to keep the leak from gaining. In the interval the masts had been cut away, and the light hamper of the upper deck torn off. At 8 A.M. the gunboat Bienville *bore down to them, and, having been informed of their condition, was requested to remain by them. A boat was then sent from the* Winfield Scott *to the* Bienville, *containing three disabled soldiers and a woman, the wife of one of the officers. This boat was swamped alongside the gunboat after the passengers had left it, and then the* Bienville *sent one of her life-boats to bring away some of the soldiers. After one trip, performed safely, this boat met a similar fate to the other.*

Among those, however, who left the leaking steamer on this occasion, was the Chief Engineer and his third assistant. They cowardly abandoned their posts without the shadow of an excuse. The vessel being divided into three water-tight compartments, her engines in the centre division, not a drop of water touched them, and they escaped injury, and never ceased working until the steamer dropped anchor at this place. I am glad to say that both delinquents have been returned to their vessel, where they are now confined in irons, pending the time when the punishment they deserved shall be administered. The name of the Chief Engineer, I understand, is Saven; that of the other I did not learn.

Finding that the transhipment of the men could not be accomplished by means of boats, the Bienville *ran alongside the disabled steamer and twenty of the soldiers at that time scrambled on board. The* Bienville *boarded on the port-bow, and in doing so had her gunwales carried away by catching them upon the anchor. This mode of proceeding also proving a failure, the* Bienville *contented herself by remaining by the* Scott *until three and a half o'clock P.M., by which time the weather had moderated. Some more of the soldiers making the aggregate number about forty were then taken off, when the sea becoming comparatively smooth, it was found that the steamer ceased to take in water and could be saved. Accordingly the* Bienville *left her and by nightfall she had been pumped out, her leaks stopped, and was making her way comfortably to the rendezvous. On the next evening (Sunday), the* Vanderbilt *took her in tow and brought her to the anchorage. A serious error happened during the height of the confusion on board, which I should have thought could only have resulted from a panic among the soldiers, but I am assured by the officers that the men never for a moment lost their presence of mind. When the order was given to throw the guns overboard, meaning the rifled cannon, about three hundred of the soldiers plunged their muskets into the sea, under the impression that they were obeying directions, and in their zeal it was not long before their overcoats followed their arms.*

Still the *Winfield Scott* came, battered and leaking, carrying hundreds of Pennsylvanian soldiers vowing to never leave solid ground again. The *Belvidere*, carrying horses, was disabled enough to turn back to Fortress Monroe for repairs. The *Governor*, transporting the marine battalion, had floundered and

The *Winfield Scott* losing its masts in the gale, November 1–2, 1861. *Author's collection.*

The Rescue of the *Governor*

Up until four o'clock, the Governor had done fairly well. The boat was a converted merchant steamer, which usually carried just commercial cargo and only made runs between Bangor and Boston. On November 1861, it was out on the ocean, on a trip over twice its normal length and heavily burdened with military wares and a battalion of marines while facing down a storm.

Major Reynolds, commander of the marines onboard, noted that it was about four o'clock when "we were struck by two or three heavy seas." This pounding buckled support braces on one side of the ship, bending them inward. Unable to bear the new load, braces on the other side broke off completely.

Reynolds reacted immediately. He barked out orders, and officers and enlisted men alike went to work to shore up the failing braces. Ropes were used to affix them in place. This danger had just passed when the support braces around the smokestack parted. With a loud creak, the smokestack plummeted off the side of the ship, disappearing into the swirling waters below. In the engine room, the steam pipe swelled and then burst, scalding the air with a high-pitched whine. Unable to build up a head of steam, the best the Governor could do was to creep along. In order to restore pressure, it was necessary to kill the engine completely for minutes at a time and submit to the mercy of the waves.

An hour into this predicament, some other members of the fleet were spotted driving against the gale, one boat towing another. Six rockets went up from the Governor to get their attention. It seemed to work; signals were exchanged via the flags. Then the ships disappeared behind a curtain of wind and wave. With no rockets left, the Governor's crew was forced to improvise. Reynolds ordered his men on deck, and in the driving rain, they fired volleys with their muskets into the air, hoping that the noise would draw the other two ships back to them. Periodically, the veil would part and the ships would come back into view, but the distance could not be closed. Darkness closed in around them, the ships vanished behind a curtain of water and the men on the Governor realized that they were on their own.

The steamer continued as best it could. At some point, the ship shed another chain, this one holding the rudder. Every time the boat lurched, Reynolds feared that the jury-rigged braces would be carried away. Without them, the entire starboard side was in danger of being torn out, the boiler would collapse and the wheelhouse would be lost. A detail of one hundred men was tasked with holding the braces in place through the storm. No one was sleeping in this tumult, even if they had somehow been able to. All hands were needed to keep water out of the ship. Hundreds of men performed this seemingly impossible task by bailing with buckets or using hand-powered bilge pumps.

At 3:00 a.m. the packing around the cylinder head of the engine blew out, rendering the engine completely useless. Despair must have settled over the marines as their best weapon against the weather was gone. If they despaired, it did not stop them from *expending every ounce of energy in staying afloat. They continued to work the pumps and to scoop briny water from the ship.*

The mechanics, tired and overworked already, scrambled, trying to coax life out of the inert engine. As a testament to their skill, the engine restarted but ran even slower than before.

Daybreak seemed to bring salvation. The weather was still dreadful, but the sky had brightened and the wind had lulled some. Another pair of the fleet was spotted nearby. Once again, flags were dipped and words passed silently over the waves. At 10:00 a.m. the Isaac Smith *hailed the* Governor. *Seeing the condition of their boat, the* Governor's *crew was advised to abandon it and come aboard the* Smith. *The* Smith *put out a small boat; it was rowed over, and a thick coil of rope, called a hawser, was flung up to the* Governor. *Relief was short-lived. Reynolds stated that the hawser, "through the carelessness of Captain C.L. Litchfield, of the* Governor, *was soon cast off or unavoidably let go."*

It was one o'clock before a second hawser could be procured and transported from the Smith. *This time, the* Governor *was able to secure the ropes to the* Smith. *Rescue was snatched from them yet again. Under the strain of pulling another ship's weight, the hawser parted. The* Governor *slid back into the ocean, its engine sputtering, alone again.*

The other boat, the Young Rover, *soon put in an appearance. It signaled a reassuring message to the* Governor's *crew. It would stay by their boat to the last. This message was relayed to the soaked, bleary-eyed marines, who sent up an exuberant cheer at the expression of loyalty. They got even better news from the* Young Rover. *Although the* Governor *couldn't see it, a third ship of the fleet, a large frigate, was in the* Young Rover's *line of vision. It had relayed their plight and the frigate had changed course to respond.*

It was two or three o'clock when the Sabine *came into view. Captain Ringgold of that boat described the scene as he came upon it:*

> A side-wheel steamer, rolling heavily, rudder gone, smokestack overboard, her decks crowded with human beings, lay before me, a helpless wreck, and a small screw steamer, evidently much damaged and scarcely able to take care of herself, was nobly standing by her in her misfortune.

The Sabine *was not a member of the fleet—it was a blockader sailing down the Georgetown coast in execution of its duty. Providentially, it had spotted the* Young Rover. *Reynolds noted, "Hope once more cheered the hearts of all on board the transport." Captain Ringgold let them know that he would do everything in his power to get them off their dying ship. They were past the point where they could be towed to port. The exhausted marines were losing the fight against the water; several feet of it had seeped into the ship and it was rising.*

A third hawser and then three more and an iron stream cable made their way over to the Governor, *binding the two ships together. The* Sabine *dropped anchor, and to secure its*

Triumphant Still Their Course Southward Lay

position, the Governor *followed suit. The weather, which had improved, had still not settled. It was between eight and nine o'clock before the* Sabine *had played out enough chain to make a rescue attempt. Reynolds recalled:*

> The *Sabine* had paid out enough chain to bring her stern close to our bow. Spars were rigged out over the stern of the frigate and every arrangement made for whipping our men on board, and some thirty men were rescued by this means.

The plunging of the vessels strained the support lines and then snapped four of them.
Three feet of water was in the holds, and the men were so tired that they could barely stand. Desperation drove the next rescue attempt. Reynolds offers the following eyewitness testimony as the rescue attempt escalated into a potential disaster:

> It was evidently intended by the commanding officer of the *Sabine* to get the *Governor* alongside and let our men jump from the boat to the frigate. In our condition this appeared extremely hazardous. It seemed impossible for us to strike the frigate without instantly going to pieces. We were, however, brought alongside and some forty men succeeded in getting on board the frigate. One was crushed to death between the frigate and the steamer in attempting to gain a foothold on the frigate. Shortly after being brought alongside the frigate the starboard quarter off the *Sabine* struck the port bow of the *Governor*, and carried away about 20 feet of the hurricane deck from the stem to the wheelhouse.
>
> The sea was running so high, and we being tossed—so violently, it was deemed prudent to slack up the hawser and let the *Governor* fall astern of the frigate with the faint hope of weathering the gale till morning. All our provisions and other stores, indeed every movable article, were thrown overboard, and the water casks started to lighten the vessel. From half past 3 until daybreak the *Governor* floated in comparative safety, notwithstanding the water was rapidly gaining on her. At daybreak preparations were made for sending boats to our relief, although the sea was running high, and it being exceedingly dangerous for a boat to approach the guards of the steamer. In consequence the boats laid off and the men were obliged to jump into the sea, and were then hauled into the boats. All hands were thus providentially rescued from the wreck with the

exception, I am pained to say, of 1 corporal and 6 privates, who were drowned or killed by the crush or contact of the vessels. Those drowned were lost through their disobedience of orders in leaving the tanks, or abandoning their posts.

In his report, Captain Ringgold provides another view of this incident:

While alongside, two marines in their attempts to reach the ship fell between the vessels and one was crushed to death. As she fell astern, six others in the panic leaped overboard in the hope of gaining the ship and were drowned. Here succeeded a scene that beggars description; the despair felt on feeling this attempt at rescue had proved so unsuccessful, the bubbling cry of drowning men. the confusion on board the wreck, the unnatural glare of the sea and sky, caused by the rockets and the red and blue lights (signals for assistance to the *Isaac Smith* and *Young Rover*), presented a scene that might well have struck terror to the stoutest heart.

With the men taken care of, they turned their attention to salvage. Jettisoned cargo from the Governor *was pulled back onto the* Sabine. *Through a herculean effort, half of the* Governor's *stores was saved. In his official report on the incident, Reynolds extolled the virtues of his rescuers, especially Captain Ringgold:*

Under God, we owe our preservation to Captain Ringgold and the officers of the *Sabine*, to whom we tender our heartfelt thanks

Triumphant Still Their Course Southward Lay

> for their untiring labors while we were in danger and their unceasing kindness since we have been on board the frigate.

He saved special thanks for his own command:

> Too much praise can not be bestowed upon the officers and men under my command. All did nobly. The firmness with which they performed their duty is beyond all praise. For forty eight hours they stood at ropes and passed water to keep the ship afloat. Refreshments in both eating and drinking were passed to them at their posts by noncommissioned officers.

Three hours later, the Governor's *death throes ceased; it was claimed by the victorious sea. The* Sabine *put in for Port Royal. Reynolds requisitioned from the crew of the blockader eight men to replace those he had lost. Time was not on their side. By the time they anchored off Port Royal, the battle had been decided. The marines of the* Governor *would return to Hampton Roads a few days later on another steamer. Although they did not take part in the fight of November 7, their story of survival remains an integral part of the Port Royal Expedition.*

gone under, but its crew and half of its cargo were saved by the actions of other members of the fleet, especially the *Sabine*.

The big secret was now revealed. The scattering of the fleet was the contingency Du Pont had prepared for. Waxed seals were broken, and the captains could be secure at least of a rendezvous point, if not much else.

Du Pont trusted that his orders were clear and explicit. The *Wabash* would continue toward its destination. The fleet never regained the grand formation it had shown at Hampton Roads. Remnants of the fleet advanced toward Port Royal in small clusters and in single file. But it did continue, and in great strength. The storm had been a setback but had not dealt the fleet a cataclysmic blow.

As if spent, the weather quieted. On Sunday, November 3, at 9:40 p.m., Davis logged, "The sky and sea have been growing milder, and tonight....the weather is most beautiful...We are standing in for Port Royal and will anchor soon outside the bar." By November 4, the *Wabash* and twenty-five other members of the fleet were safely stationed outside Port Royal. More ships were spotted straggling down the coast.

The Tragedy Off Charleston

After the great storm, the Wabash *and the* Seneca *sailed a little farther west, coming into the cordon of blockaders stationed off Charleston. Before departing Hampton Roads, Du Pont had sent a message to Captain Lardner. His ship, the* Susquehanna, *was to be pulled from its duty watching the Charleston approaches and added to the fleet. "Tell no one of my coming," Du Pont had ordered, and apparently this silence was honored. The other blockaders were taken aback at the appearance of their brethren.*

This was a short layover; to repair from the delay caused by the storm they needed to swiftly continue on their way. During this brief period, the fleet lost another member tragically. According to an eyewitness: "We were aloft furling sails, when a cap blew off and was carried into the water; down went the blue-jacket who owned it." The sailor, William Emmet, had tucked inside this cap a treasured memento—a picture of his love. Emmet ran to the starboard gangway and sprang overboard, determined to save the picture. "Man overboard was shouted, and a boat was ordered to be lowered, before the boat could be lowered…the officer of the deck, who had divested himself of his sword and coat, jumped overboard." This brave officer was Lieutenant Stephen B. Luce. Emmet was floundering, and Luce swam out valiantly to rescue him. Sadly, the water claimed Emmet. "Those of us who were still aloft were now alarmed for the safety of the officer as we saw large numbers of hideous sharks around him." The sailors in the rigging yelled and pointed, alerting Luce to his predicament, which action caused him to pick up the pace and keep going.

Luce returned safely to the Wabash. *Emmet was never seen again and "without a doubt was seized and carried down by the sharks." Luce would serve through the Port Royal campaign and had a long and distinguished career in the navy, reaching the rank of rear admiral. He is also credited as the founder of the Naval War College. After he had retired from the service, one member of his former command who had been present that day wrote:*

> I say Dear Admiral Luce for the reason I can only look back to the dark days of '61, and remember you with feelings of admiration and respect akin even to affection…I was in the *Wabash* with you, and well do remember the day when lying off Charleston you jumped off…and attempted to save poor Bill Emmett: what a noble deed for you.

CHAPTER 4

Those Shores So Serene

Perhaps the first intimation that Port Royal would be the target of a large-scale attack came on August 29, 1861. This warning was telegraphed by Ambrose Gonzales, a Cuban revolutionary who had joined the Confederate cause and rose to the rank of officer. Two forts in Cape Hatteras had been taken by a joint army and naval force in August, and with unnerving prescience, this skilled engineer predicted that Port Royal would be the next point of attack. In September, he wrote to a friend that he was "very anxious about Port Royal." To the best of his ability, Gonzales funneled ordnance, in great demand everywhere, into South Carolina.

When confirmation came that Port Royal was indeed the intended objective of the October fleet, Gonzales drew upon his considerable organizational and logistical talents. While in Charleston, eighty men, mostly wealthy aristocrats from the leading families of the Carolina Lowcountry—Jervey, Elliott, Buist and Trenholm—were mustered into an emergency force. By rail, they rushed to Port Royal, bringing along the powder and cartridges that Gonzales had appropriated. However, they did not depart Charleston until Friday, November 8, the day after the battle had been decided. They would miss the action at Port Royal, but some would participate in the later engagement at Port Royal Ferry.

News of the fleet's departure had long since reached Charleston, and speculation of its ultimate destination set the telegraph wires buzzing and letter writers guessing. Thomas Elliott responded to family concerns that the fleet would be coming to Beaufort: "It will not be for the purpose of taking the Town

Beaufort

Beaufort was founded in the early eighteenth century, circa 1711. This makes it the second-oldest city, behind Charleston, in South Carolina. Like a number of localities in the Carolinas, it was named in tribute to English aristocracy; in this case, Henry Somerset, the second Duke of Beaufort. Somerset helped operate the colony as one of the Lords Proprietors, a select group of gentlemen who governed in the name of the king of England.

Beaufort began as a military outpost to guard against Spanish excursions. As the closest city to Spanish-held St. Augustine, it was literally the southern frontier of the British Empire. The town was torched in 1715 during a fierce war against a coalition of disaffected Native Americans that came to be known as the Yamassee War.

The town was rebuilt, expanded and flourished. Its prosperity was due in large part to the rich plantations operating in its vicinity. In the period right before the Civil War, the town became a summer retreat—the so-called sickly season—for the Sea Island cotton planters. Historian Lawrence Rowland offers the following snapshot of Beaufort in 1860: "By 1860 Beaufort was one of the wealthiest towns in America and a center of the secession movement."

Beaufort faced one of its greatest trials during the Battle of Port Royal and the subsequent Federal occupation. Homes were lost, businesses destroyed and the rules of society were turned upside-down. The residents had to draw on their ancestral reservoir of strength to reshape Beaufort into the thriving southern city it remains today.

Beaufort, 1865. *Library of Congress.*

of Beaufort. It is to possess and occupy Hilton Head as a strategic point—for the war, that they will assail Port Royal."

On November 2, Governor Francis Pickens of South Carolina was sure that the blow would fall in the Palmetto State. He telegraphed the Confederate secretary of war, Judah Benjamin, for assistance. Benjamin was unable to do more than promise aid when it appeared that South Carolina was indeed under attack.

Why Not Charleston?

Charleston, founded in 1670 as Charles Towne, was one of the most prosperous cities in the United States by the time of the Civil War. The events that took place within its boundaries and in its harbor in 1860 and '61 transformed it into a prime military and political target. In the closing days of December 1860, the city hosted the Secession Convention, in which South Carolina seceded from the Union. Charleston drew the attention of the nation again on April 9, 1861, when the Federal garrison in Fort Sumter was fired upon by the Confederates. To conquer and humble this birthplace of secession and the Civil War would be a great coup for the Federals. However, it would not be an easy task. Numerous forts like Sumter, Moultrie and Johnson, along with innumerable coastal batteries, shielded the city, and reinforcements could be rushed to fill its streets via one of the railroad lines running into the city. These factors rendered Charleston a tougher-caliber opponent than the Blockade Board was willing to take on in November 1861.

In a November 3, 1861 letter, Caroline Howard Gilman tells of how the fleet's approach caused anxiety, but not panic, in Charleston: "This is the most agitating periods of the war, as the Great Fleet is momentarily expected…The buoyancy of our people is wonderful and so calm too."

Gilman also offers a glimpse into some of the preparations in Charleston, specifically the outfitting of a transport:

> *The* Gordon *had begun its life as an armed steamer. In October of 1861 it had been stripped of its guns, dressed with flowers and rechristened* Theodora. *This boat ran the blockade, carrying from Charleston Confederate diplomats James Mason and John Slidell* [whose eventual capture would cause the famous Trent Affair] *to Nassau. The* Theodora *slid back through the blockade having exchanged its human cargo for one of pistols, swords, lead, coffee and 200,000 cigars!*

These welcome items were promptly unloaded, and Gilman recalled the ship's next tour of duty:

> *In view of the expected attack at Bay Point, near Beaufort, by the Lincoln Fleet, she was engaged immediately upon her arrival as a transport. Gilman's sons, Frank and Willie went down to the wharf and worked with twenty men and four drays all night to get the ship in order for its next task. A telegraph just announces that two of the Lincoln transports are aground off Georgetown, but they can afford to lose a few.*

The Battle of Port Royal

Hilton Head

Although the Native Americans were there first and William Hilton explored the area over one hundred years after the evacuation of the Spanish from the area, this large island bordering the Atlantic Ocean bears his name. Its remote location and proximity to Spanish Florida put it in a dangerous sector, contributing to the fact that it took fifty-four years for the first white settler to put up a permanent residence on the island. Numerous sprawling plantations, owned by the local gentry, dotted the island at the time of the Port Royal Expedition. Tens of thousands of Federals were stationed on Hilton Head over the course of the Civil War. The old properties on Hilton Head were abandoned after the Confederate evacuation and fell into disuse. It was not until the twentieth century that Hilton Head had a resurgence as a popular resort community.

On November 2, word had begun to filter down to Beaufort that the fleet was headed in their direction, having bypassed Charleston. Emily Walker Barnwell, a resident of the area, remembered the precautions taken by her family: "Saturday I went around to grandma's. Aunt Sarah decided she would pack up the books. Daddy Will, the butler, brought in the boxes, we filled them and he nailed them up."

The next day, William Oliver Perry Fripp attended his usual Sunday service at the Chapel of Ease on St. Helena Island. Unfortunately, it would not be a day of prayer and reflection. A mounted messenger sought Fripp out and informed him that the fleet had sailed past Charleston. It was likely that the fleet would not pass Port Royal Sound. As captain of the St. Helena Mounted Volunteer Riflemen, Fripp was ordered to commandeer all "Negroes, boats and floats, and have them at the most convenient point to bring off our soldiers from Bay Point should it be necessary for them to retreat." Precautions were already underway to make sure that the defenders were not to be hemmed in the forts, should Walker and Beauregard fall, and the men could survive to fight another day. Fripp rushed from church and sent word to his men to assemble these items and rally at Seaside Plantation.

Across town at the St. Helena Church, Ann Barnwell Mazyck joined the other parishioners in singing an impassioned version of the tune "God Save the South." Upon its conclusion, Reverend Walker told the congregation what they already knew: that the army was coming heavily into the area and the fleet was at their doorstep. The next day at noon, he said, he would ring the church bells, and he hoped that the congregation would gather at that time in their homes for prayer.

Even in faraway Norfolk, they had surmised the fleet's destination. On Monday, November 4, "the Yankee fleet were preparing to land at Port Royal."

CHAPTER 5

WHERE HILTON HEAD AND LOW BAY POINT DEFIED

It may have been fresh from its wharf-side christening, but the *Seneca* had survived the storm intact. Captain Ammen reported no casualties and no major damage. The new crew could scratch a notch on its raw hull. Now they knew the measure of the ship; some of its hidden quirks had surfaced under the stress of hard sailing.

Daylight broke over a sea still hemorrhaging from the frenzy of the night before, albeit at a much slower pace. It was as if an angry challenger had overturned the chessboard, scattering the playing pieces out of one another's reach. The morning sun rose a little higher, gradually revealing another sail on the horizon. It was the *Wabash*. The fleet might have lacked a king in this game, and numerous pawns had already been sacrificed, but its queen was still in play.

The majestic warship signaled to Ammen at eight o'clock. It required his presence. The boats dropped anchors; Ammen was rowed over to the flagship and hauled up. A short conference with Du Pont followed. No doubt, the storm was discussed. Nevertheless, the important topic of the day was where they were headed next. Du Pont was adamant: Port Royal was their destination. There was no turning back. He believed that the fleet was still in a condition to achieve its objective; the missing ships were bound to arrive, and the battle would go on with whatever remained.

The *Wabash* would skirt Charleston while continuing south. Ammen was ordered to take the *Seneca* into the blockade cordon around Charleston. There, he was to find Captain J.L. Lardner of the *Susquehanna*. Lardner had received a telegram days ago from Du Pont and knew that this meeting was coming. His ship was to be pulled off the blockade and its armament added to the Port Royal Expedition. The Confederates had even let him know that this time was approaching. While he was on the water, away from telegraph wires, newspapers and current events, the inhabitants of Charleston were not. They had gotten news that the fleet was on the move. Lardner must have described to Ammen, as he did to Du Pont the next day, how Tuesday had been a flurry of activity for Charleston. The forts ringing the city practiced their gunnery. At night, lit barrels of tar were set adrift in the harbor with a hope that these would illuminate the fleet if it descended upon them.

Ammen bade his farewells and crossed the trackless path back to his ship. Based on their charts and reckonings, Charleston lay thirty miles to the south. The weather held. Ammen was able to get into the blockade network later that afternoon. A sharp-eyed gunner in Fort Sumter spotted the enemy ship. It fired a cannon to announce the presence of a new Federal interloper. This cannon was acknowledged with another discharge farther in the heavily guarded harbor. The city where secession had become a reality girded itself. Ammen arranged a face-to-face with Captain Lardner in order to relay their superior's directions verbally. No sense in giving those Confederates hunkered over the walls, peering with spyglasses, a chance to decipher their seaborne signals.

When darkness settled thickly over the harbor, blanketing watchful eyes around Charleston, the *Seneca* and the *Susquehanna* maneuvered away from the city, following the wake of the *Wabash*. The next day, the two ships were anchored off Port Royal, part of a fleet undergoing steady resurrection.

Du Pont knew that it was important to maintain order on a ship. Occurrences like the storm had to be blips in a carefully maintained regime. Although they were in extraordinary circumstances, twenty-five miles off Charleston and with much of the fleet still AWOL, they would honor the Sabbath as they did every Sunday. Holding regular church service on the *Wabash* was important to Du Pont for other reasons. His wife, Sophie, was a devout Episcopalian and had brought her husband into that faith. The two were founders of the Christ Church Christiana Hundred in Delaware.

Du Pont wrote to Sophie about that particular service:

> *We had a nice service…with an excellent sermon, I think; no special adaptation to sailors but still interesting, on the ministrations of angels. I thought they listened with great attention, and the chaplain's concluding prayer afterwards touched very well upon pending events. Indeed, precious, these are at hand and*

Where Hilton Head and Low Bay Point Defied

JOHN WAGENER AND THE FORT WALKER FLAG

March 4, 2004

The inhabitants of this historic Robert Mills structure, the South Carolina Historical Society (SCHS), were generally a fairly predictable lot. Staff arrived between 8:00 and 8:30 a.m.; researchers started assembling under the columns of the Fireproof Building about 9:00 a.m.; and by 4:00 p.m. the last of this group of hopefuls had been ushered out. By 5:30 p.m., the staff had departed, the doors were closed for the last time that day, the exterior lights were flipped on and the windows were securely shuttered. The Fireproof Building's original 1826 design called for metal shutters, and the SCHS saw no reason to alter Mills's vision. Twin metal shutters covered the tall, arched windows that looked out from unlit rooms, projecting the illusion that the building was soundly asleep.

Tonight, the Fireproof Building was anything but asleep. The oppressive shutters were pulled back, the exterior and interior lights were turned all the way up and crowds of people, talking and laughing, were clearly visible moving around inside. They had gathered to witness an event that had never taken place in the history of the SCHS, a notable landmark in itself considering how much the SCHS had experienced since its 1855 founding. On this Thursday evening, a banner of the Confederacy, lost to the South since 1861, was coming home.

Major John A. Wagener's exact location on the evening of December 20, 1860, is unknown. As a resident of Charleston, and as a civic leader, it is likely that he was part of the multitude that witnessed secession transform from political abstraction into reality. If

The Fort Walker flag as it appeared in 2004. *From the South Carolina Historical Society.*

he had indeed ventured out of his George Street address to bear witness to the ratification of the Ordinance of Secession, it was solely from a sense of public duty. The Charleston streets were swept that night with a riotous crowd that cheered and celebrated this historic sundering. On practically every street corner, over-enthusiastic individuals had gleefully peppered the buildings with innumerable "The Union is Dissolved" handbills.

For Wagener, this was something to be mourned, not championed. Based on the writings of those who knew him, he belonged to a minority within Charleston; his sympathies were for the fallen Union. Wagener was well read, and as one of the pillars of the community in Charleston—he moved in high circles—he surely saw this political break looming like a storm cloud over the future of his adopted country. Despite his objections to secession, Wagener would go to war to defend it. One of Wagener's biographers summed up his decision:

> However much Wagener supported the Union and regretted the impulse to separate, South Carolina had become his real home. Here was his property; here his children were born; in short, here was everything that bound him to the earth; and from this state he received his officer rank.

Wagener had left Germany nearly three decades earlier. In 1833, while in his mid-teens, he became a member of the venerable German Fusiliers. In 1837, Governor Butler appointed Wagener lieutenant of the German Riflemen. Six years later, Governor Hammond promoted Wagener again, this time as first lieutenant of the German Fusiliers. In 1847, Governor Johnson granted him the rank of captain. In recognition of his civic contributions and service, a fourth governor, Governor Gist, had conferred the rank of major of the Second Battalion of the First Artillery Regiment of South Carolina.

The regiment was activated when the Federal garrison under Major Robert Anderson moved from Fort Moultrie to occupy Fort Sumter on December 26, 1860. The abandoned Fort Moultrie had to be retaken. But Anderson couldn't be trusted any longer; his move to Sumter was viewed as a betrayal, and upon leaving he had set ablaze the gun carriages. When civilian laborers, who had been formerly employed by Anderson, claimed that Moultrie might have been laced with mines, the threat was taken seriously. The artillery experts were called out to retake the fort safely.

This rumor turned out to be false. Fort Moultrie was safely occupied by Confederate troops. Wagener and the soldiers of the German Artillery stayed on alert through the rest of the Fort Sumter crisis. Detachments were placed throughout the harbor when cadets from The Citadel fired on the Star of the West from Morris Island in early January. A month later, Wagener was in command of Castle Pinckney.

This military post was a castle in title only. In reality, it was a second system masonry fort on an island out in Charleston Harbor. Like many of the forts of that era, it was named

Where Hilton Head and Low Bay Point Defied

after a war hero of the past; the name Pinckney came from Charles Cotesworth Pinckney, a celebrated veteran of the Revolutionary War, author, signer of the Constitution and one of the participants of the XYZ Affair.

In recent years, the fort had been delegated as of secondary importance. Its heyday had been in 1812, when Charlestonians worried that a British fleet would arrive to burn their city, just as it had Washington, D.C. The British never fulfilled that fear. Castle Pinckney saw no action in that war, and the fort fell into relative disuse until tensions became strained between federal and state governments during the nullification crisis of 1832, when it was regarrisoned.

By 1860, the squat fort on the low sandy island only three-quarters of a mile from the city had become nearly obsolete until Anderson's move gave it renewed importance. Governor Pickens had ordered it captured. Although Pinckney was too close to the city to be much of a factor in the coming contest, it offered a buffer against attacks from the Mount Pleasant side to Charleston and, perhaps more importantly, served as a psychological buffer from the Federal forces. It was during this period that Major Wagener and the group of officers began to remark that their post needed its own distinctive flag.

The cadre of officers was thinking on a grand scale, as was evidenced by the write-up it received in the February 1 edition of the Charleston Mercury. *Under the heading "Matters at Castle Pinckney," it was reported:*

> A beautiful new flag was run up the staff this morning. The design is unique and showy, and was devised and purchased by the officers of the garrison. Two white palmettos are blazoned upon a red field, with a crescent between them and fifteen stars in an arch above, with alternate stripes of blue and red and white, as in the Federal flag.

The Charleston Courier *run on the same day was much less profuse, simply stating that "Major J.A. Wagener, the gallant Commandant at this post has given to the breeze a Garrison Flag—A beautiful banner of fifteen stars."*

The flag was ten by twelve feet in dimension; two bright red palmettos were stitched on it, along with fifteen stars and fifteen blue and white stripes. Modern-day historians think that the two palmetto trees symbolized the belief held by many Southerners that the coming trials would be their second war for independence. It is assumed that Wagener, with the other Castle Pinckney officers, commissioned a Charleston merchant named Hugh E. Vincent, who dealt in ship supplies, for the task of making this flag a reality. This was after South Carolina's secession, but before the first shots were fired at Fort Sumter and before the first national flag was adopted.

On April 9, 1861, Wagener was summoned back to Fort Moultrie, where his skill was needed to force the evacuation of Fort Sumter. It is unknown if the new flag flew from

The Battle of Port Royal

Castle Pinckney, which only marked the bombardment but did not participate, or if it was transferred to Fort Moultrie for this occasion.

For nearly a day and a half, the cannons placed strategically in the harbor fired on Sumter. Moultrie's cannons spewed "hotshot" onto their target. Furnaces had been set up across Sullivan's Island to supply the attacking positions with these cannonballs, which had been cooked until red hot. The touch of this super-heated metal upon wood would generally produce fire. It would be these hotshots that would help to ultimately do Sumter in. Fire threatened the main magazine of the fort, and Anderson simply did not have the means to combat it.

Wagener would have been in position to personally witness the first blockading vessel. The USS Niagara arrived in May to stop any maritime traffic to Charleston. The lone vessel did little to close the port and was the subject of much ridicule in the Charleston papers.

In July, Wagener was promoted to lieutenant colonel in the CSA army, with orders to raise a company of German volunteers. Not only did Wagener recruit the necessary men, but he also furnished a large sum of the funds needed to equip the company, dubbed "the German Volunteers," out of his own pocket. Captain W.K. Bachman, who had accompanied Wagener on the December 27 trip to Moultrie, was selected to head the unit. Henry Wagener, one of John's sons, also joined the unit. The German volunteers were shipped to Virginia, where they would play a part in many key battles, including Gettysburg and Fredericksburg.

Wagener was promoted to colonel of the First South Carolina Artillery Regiment on July 24, 1861.

When John Wagener returned to duty in Charleston, the number of hostile ships off of Charleston had increased drastically. Eleven warships made a regular circuit of Savannah, Charleston and the North Carolina coast.

In September, Fort Walker and Fort Beauregard were in sufficient shape to receive their armaments. Wagener's unit was called to oversee placement and aid in the defense. A memento of home was going with them. Before leaving Castle Pinckney, the flag was hauled down, and Wagener carried it to Port Royal with him. It was from this post that the flag would later come to be called "the Fort Walker Flag."

While prowling the battered Fort Walker, Commodore John Rodgers happened upon an officer's sword hanging in a tent. He also found Wagener's flag. This he used to wrap the appropriated sword, and both were given to his superior and hero of the Battle of Port Royal, Commander Du Pont. Interestingly enough, in a letter to his wife, Rodgers describes the sword in detail but only makes an off-hand mention of this "Secession Flag." Du Pont, in turn, sent the flag to the Department of the Navy. In honor of George Washington's birthday in February 1862, a collection of war trophies—specifically banners and flags captured from the Confederates—was put on display in the Old Capitol Building in Washington, D.C.

On August 12, 1869, Captain Gustavus V. Fox donated the flag to the Massachusetts Historical Society. It remained in the society's keeping until June 2003, when that

Where Hilton Head and Low Bay Point Defied

> *organization de-accessioned it, gifting it to the South Carolina Historical Society. The SCHS reached out to the community and its members and raised the funds necessary to get the Fort Walker flag properly conserved and a protective case built.*
>
> *In an interview about the ceremony, William Fowler, executive director of the Massachusetts Historical Society, related how a representative of South Carolina made a visit to Lexington, Massachusetts, in 1876. The purpose of the visit was to return the flag that had fallen with the Fifty-fourth Massachusetts on its ill-fated charge on Battery Wagner out on Morris Island in 1863. (While Sergeant Carney had saved the national colors, the state colors had been torn from the staff and held by CSA General Ripley until 1875.) "It seems to me that we have been late in reciprocating that gesture," Fowler stated. "These are flags, icons, historical reminders that ought to be shared. They're American treasures, and Americans ought to see them."*
>
> *The Fort Walker flag is on permanent display on the third floor of the South Carolina Historical Society's headquarters at 100 Meeting Street in Charleston. It is part of a brief guided tour of the archives, which is free to members of the SCHS and open to the general public for a small fee.*

> *I cannot but feel thankful that another Sabbath will be unattended with scenes that would do violence to its spirit and beneficent ordering.*

Since sending Ammen on his errand, he had made contact with several of the steamers. Seven ships were accounted for—a small amount when compared to the original number, yet enough to give hope that more had endured, opened their sealed letters and were racing to join them. He was sure that "by tomorrow, they will draw in, as if into a funnel."

At 8:00 p.m. they reached a spot thirty-five miles from where the light vessel near Port Royal formally stood. These mobile, floating lighthouses were stationed at points where building a lighthouse was untenable. Of course, the Confederates were not going to light the way for the invaders. Precautions were taken upon news of the fleet's departure. From Cape Henry to the Rio Grande, the light vessels had been removed, the lighthouses darkened and the beacons, buoys and other navigational tools pulled up. The fleet would proceed cautiously, relying heavily on their guide, Mr. Boutelle.

Twenty-four hours later, the *Wabash* was anchored in nine fathoms, with the entrance to Port Royal in sight. Captain Ammen offers his impression of the same view:

> *The bar of Port Royal lies ten miles from the nearest low sandy shores which form the land-locked harbor; only the tops of the taller trees are*

The Tragedy of Dr. Buist

Union General T.W. Sherman noted the following in a report to his superiors:

> On clearing out the fort at Hilton Head the dead body of Dr. Buist, formerly an assistant surgeon in the Army, was found in one of the galleries...he having been killed by the explosion of a shell and buried by the falling in of a parapet. He was the principal surgeon of this fort.

Dr. Edwin Somers Buist was born to Reverend E.T. Buist of Greenville, South Carolina, in 1837. At twenty-two years of age, he attended the University of Virginia as a student. He was noted as being more of a "concrete" than abstract thinker and possessed "good practical judgment."

Buist studied the sciences at the university to prepare himself to enter his chosen career as a doctor. In 1857, he transferred to the University of New York and graduated from the medical department in 1859. A tour of the Southwest left him with a desire to relocate to Arkansas. Secession and the outbreak of the Civil War kept him in Charleston, where he practiced medicine. Although a native, Buist did not advocate secession, but he would stand by his state should it choose to pursue this course of action.

When South Carolina called for volunteers, Buist was as good as his word. He enlisted and served as assistant surgeon of the Ninth South Carolina Infantry and Colonel Wagener's German Artillery. In the latter part of 1861, he transferred with his command to Hilton Head, into Fort Walker. During the November 7 bombardment, Buist set up his operating table in one of the covered passages in the fort in order to be close to the wounded. He was attending to a patient when he was struck by heavy shell fire, which caused the passageway to collapse around him.

While clearing out the fort, the Federal soldiers came across the remains of Buist and his unidentified patient. A postwar biographical sketch done by the University of Virginia stated that Buist's body "was found beneath a mass of sand and timber, on the attitude of ligating the temporal artery of a soldier, and still grasping the tenaculum [a slender hooked instrument used in surgery] in his hand."

Dr. Edward Dalton of New York took possession of Buist's body. Dalton was a surgeon in the Federal fleet and had been a friend of Buist. Dalton enlisted the aid of Dr. George Cooper, medical director of Sherman's corps, to have the remains interred. The body was buried in a makeshift coffin, a converted gun box, and laid to rest in the ground at Port Royal, his grave site marked with a headboard. His personal effects—a watch, papers, etc.—were carefully taken off the body and gently stored in

Where Hilton Head and Low Bay Point Defied

a box. Out of a show of respect to their fallen foe, the Federals buried Buist with full military honors. Every surgeon serving as part of the Port Royal Expedition attended the service.

Shortly thereafter, the family of Dr. Buist sought to reclaim their relative's mortal remains. Diarist Emma Holmes's December 3, 1861 entry gives the following information about this event:

> Cousin Willie told us that Mr. John Gourdin had read him a letter from Henry Young, who, as one of Gen. Thomas F. Drayton's aides, had gone to Port Royal with the relatives of Dr. E.L. Buist to search for his body under a flag of truce.

The Federals obliged but felt it only proper that Dr. Buist not be carried back home by his family in a rude gun box. The family was asked to wait while Dr. Buist was disinterred and put into a proper coffin. Ten hours after they had arrived, the Buist family was traveling back home with Buist's personal belongings and his corpse, gently ensconced in a freshly hewn coffin. He was given a second burial in a Charleston graveyard, where he remains today, one of the forgotten heroes of the Battle of Port Royal.

FLAG OF TRUCE FROM THE CONFEDERATES FOR A SUSPENSION OF FIRING, TO BURY THEIR DEAD, AT PORT ROYAL, S. C.

visible, except in certain states of the atmosphere when the mirage brings up to view continuous forests on Hilton Head to the west, and Bay Point in the east side of the harbor.

Barely visible at this distance, at the extreme terminus point of land, were the twin protectors of the sound, Forts Walker and Beauregard. The log and sod bastions had been called by a Confederate "the Holy watchtowers of our cause."

Eight or nine vessels were already with the *Wabash*. The horizon sported a heartening view, with plenty more sails coming in. Rather than remain idle, Du Pont ordered Mr. Boutelle into action. The surveyor jumped ship and transferred over to the nimble survey craft, the *Vixen*, under Charles Davis, that had brought him from New York. With the assistance of several other vessels, a safe route was soon determined. Du Pont applauded their efforts:

The Legacy of Sergeant Jasper, Julius Wagener and J.F. Carlsen

The fleet focused its fire first on Fort Walker, deemed the stronger of the two works. Although most of the garrison had never been in battle before, it held up well in the face of a frightful onslaught, one that would have tried even the most hardened veterans. The green troops were determined to stand their ground. Proof of their valor is seen in their determination to keep Walker's guns firing as long as possible and in some extraordinary measures performed by two of the men.

In nineteenth-century warfare, the flag was still an important psychological rallying point in the field and in the fort. It was considered noble and brave to rescue a downed banner. When the Confederate flag atop Walker was shot down, a Mr. Carlsen of the German Artillery risked his life to return it to its position on the ramparts, while shot and shell rained around him. When the South Carolina flag, the Palmetto Banner, toppled, Julius Wagener, a fifteen-year-old boy in the ranks, rushed to return it to its place. Aboard an army transport, another youth, a sixteen-year-old private, Elbridge Copp, watched this scene through a field glass:

> The flag upon Fort Walker went down, shot away by well directed aim. It was thought the Fort had surrendered and cheer after cheer went up throughout the fleet, but soon the flag made its appearance again, placed there by some daring successor of Sergeant Jasper.

Where Hilton Head and Low Bay Point Defied

Although Copp hailed from New Hampshire, he was evidently familiar with the Battle of Fort Moultrie in 1776. In that year, the Patriot defenders of that fort had dealt the British the first decisive defeat of the American Revolution. During the engagement, the flag of the fort was shot away, and Sergeant William Jasper secured his immortality by rescuing and replanting the fallen flag.

Colonel Wagener recognized the deeds of Carlsen and Private Julius Wagener in his official report. Julius Wagener did have a family connection to his commanding officer—Colonel Wagener was his father. The senior Wagener did not let fears of nepotism stop him from mentioning his son's conduct:

> Private Julius Wagener, a boy of only fifteen years of age, who replanted our noble Palmetto banner…I would not have mentioned his name, he being my own son, but for the opinion that he may hereafter become very useful to his country.

On December 19, 1861, the South Carolina House of Representatives passed a resolution to honor the young man's daring deed:

> Whereas Julius Wagener…of the 1st Regiment of Artillery, S.C. did in the battle of Fort Walker demean himself with a gallantry and a heroism worthy of the highest commendation and which reflects honor on the land of his adoption, having replaced the flag of his country after it had been shot down by the enemy; therefore
>
> Resolved, That the said Julius Wagener…is hereby appointed a State cadet and that the Board of Visitors of the State military academy be respectfully requested to receive him as an appointee of the state in that institution.

This prestigious appointment gave Julius a free ride into the institution that would become The Citadel. Julius served through the rest of the Civil War with those closer to his age. During the Spanish-American War, he served with the rank of major. He died in 1917. His obituary read, "He was a patriotic citizen, and his death will be deeply regretted."

C.F. Carlsen would serve in the German Artillery until 1864, when he proved his bravery again by volunteering to join the crew of a top-secret weapon called the Hunley. His final muster roll reads that Carlsen was "lost in the Submarine Torpedo Boat on the 16th [17th] of Feb 1864 while in the act of sinking the U.S. Steamer Housatonic."

The Battle of Port Royal

> *To the skill of Commander Davis, the fleet captain, and Mr. Boutelle, the able assistant of the coast survey, in charge of the steamer* Vixen, *the channel was immediately found, sounded out and buoyed.*

At 2:30 p.m., Du Pont got a note from Davis: "My Dear Du Pont—All the vessels of war can come in," minus the goliaths, the *Wabash* and the *Susquehanna*. The transports and bigger ships could cross in the afternoon, when the tide changed. "I am in sight of the enemy's works and shipping. All goes well. I am writing on the extremity of a vibrating cylindrical-concern."

The *Pawnee* escorted the *Curlew, Penguin, Ottawa, Seneca, Isaac Smith* and *Pembina* across the bar to safe anchorage; closer, but still a great distance below the forts. Du Pont felt a sense of pride at this accomplishment. He had started to congratulate himself when "bang, bang came the booming of a cannon." There was no gun that the Confederates could mount in those forts capable of hitting them at this distance. Who was firing at them?

***

Flag Officer Josiah Tattnall was a legend in the navy. He was born at the end of the 1700s and as a boy had faced the British on the deck of a ship in the War of 1812. Decades later, he served in the Mexican War, where he was injured. He was later presented a sword for his gallantry. His service had carried him over most of the globe, putting him in contact with the upper echelon of the sea. He had served too long under the Stars and Stripes to advocate secession, but like so many other Southerners, he could not bear the thought of fighting against his native state. Consequently, when Georgia seceded in January 1861, he resigned his commission and became a flag officer of the Confederate navy. Many of the officers and men he had served with while in the employ of the United States were now facing him on the other side.

The Confederate navy had even fewer resources than the army at its outset. It was still in its infancy when Du Pont's expedition was launched. On the morning of November 2, 1861, Tattnall received reliable information at Savannah that the enemy's fleet, which had sailed from Hampton Roads, was now lurking off Port Royal. Taking every ship he could assemble, he went to Port Royal's aid. His whole available force consisted of the paddle-steamer gun vessel *Savannah*, Lieutenant Commanding J.N. Maffitt; the *Resolute*, Lieutenant Commanding J. Pembroke Jones; the *Sampson*, Lieutenant Commanding J.S. Kennard; and the *Lady Davis*, Lieutenant Commanding J. Rutledge. These

Where Hilton Head and Low Bay Point Defied

ships formed what became known as the "Mosquito Fleet," a term, often borderline derisive, bandied about by the military when describing a small collection of boats.

To call the ships second rate was generous. The ships were inferior in many aspects to what the Federals could muster. In a letter to a friend, John Grimball, an officer on the *Lady Davis*, gives his opinion of his vessel: "The *Lady Davis* is a miserable little spit box, that is the most I can say for her with due respect for the lady after whom she is named."

Ironically, in the same letter, hearing that his friend was going to be transferred, Grimball was envious: "So you are going to Virginia, the seat of the war. I only wish I was going with you instead of being penned up here in our coast doing nothing."

Grimball was certainly doing something now. The Mosquito Fleet trekked out to make a stand against an overwhelming force of invaders in a forlorn situation akin to the Spartans at Thermopylae. Staying to the inland waterways took a little longer, but it was more secure. Undetected, the Confederate fleet reached Port Royal on Monday. It arrived in time to see a small squadron of the Federal fleet engaged near the entrance to the harbor.

Ammen, onboard the *Seneca*, wrote of the sneak attack:

> *On Monday, the 4th, this vessel entered Port Royal and sounded the channel until within 3 miles of Bay Point, when we were signaled from the* Ottawa *to return and anchor, which we did at 4 p.m. near her, about a mile farther out and a cable's length nearer the batteries. The fleet generally at this time were standing in and, anchoring.*
>
> *An hour later three rebel steamers approached us and opened fire with rifled guns, but at a distance which proved ineffective. The* Ottawa, Pembina, *and this vessel got underway, and standing in at an angle allowing our heavy guns to bear, drove them before us. At sunset we returned and anchored as before.*

A Savannah newspaper correspondent, perhaps jumbling the events of the following days with those of the fourth, wrote:

> *After a cannonading of forty minutes, during which he* [Tattnall] *succeeded in entrapping three of the enemy's "screw pelters" under the fire of our batteries, finding that he had to encounter English rifled guns he retired inside the harbor.*

The Battle of Port Royal

He couldn't see the affair—he had not gotten the reports yet—but Du Pont correctly surmised:

> The firing was from two or three small armed vessels—tugs, I suppose, of the rebels—who had run out to make a show...I think the bravado was either Poor old Commodore Tattnall from Savannah, by inside passage, or Maffitt.

A soldier in the Sixth Connecticut remembered:

> The rebel soldiers gazed at us from their strongholds, and two very scaly looking gunboats ventured down from their hiding place a short distance above the batteries, and sent us their compliments in the shape of a few shells for about the space of half an hour, but with no damage to our fleet.

A New Hampshire soldier waiting in the wings had a more sarcastic bent: "Commodore Tattnall concluding not to sink the Federal fleet, turned about and escaped up river."

The *Charleston Mercury* applauded the gallantry of Tattnall but noted that "the scene was an inspiriting one, but almost ludicrous, in the disparity of the size of the opposing fleets."

Du Pont was unimpressed by the behavior of the army's transports in this engagement. "When the firing commenced, the transports, all stopped, of course, and huddled together, like a pack of frightened chickens." To pacify the worried army officers that evening, Du Pont ordered a cordon of his gunboats to cover the transports. One of these gunboats would be stationed even farther ahead as an advance guard. From this point, a smaller boat—a launch—was let down, armed with sentries, and a blue signal light was to flash should the Mosquito Fleet try a raid during the night.

Commodore Du Pont and General Sherman conferred on the evening of the fourth. Many of the vessels essential to the army's operations were still MIA. The *Ocean Express*, in particular, contained a large cache of soldiers and needed ammunition and ordnance. As it stood, they could gather for its men only about one hundred rounds each, enough for a decent firefight but desperately wanting for a prolonged campaign. Besides the guns mounted on the ships, the soldiers would have no cannons to support them in the field. Sherman worried that the ships were permanently lost and that they would be unable to mount an offensive. He calmed his fears by focusing on the task at hand: the two forts had to be dealt with, and it appeared that the navy was going to have to do it solo.

Where Hilton Head and Low Bay Point Defied

Right: Commodore Josiah Tattnall, CSN. *Author's collection.*

Below: The CSN vessel *Lady Davis*. *Author's collection.*

This suited Du Pont just fine. From the very beginning, he had secretly harbored the hope that this would not be a joint operation but strictly a navy one. Du Pont had confided to Sophie before they had even left Hampton Roads:

> *At Port Royal the soldiers will have nothing to do—they are obliterated—though we did work out a distant landing for them when we investigated the subject; whether Sherman will agree to be a looker-on is another element.*

However, the way this expedition was structured, as long as the soldiers were on his ships, they were to be treated as sailors:

> *I am supreme in this decision, it is true, but it may be very unwise to act. If we can take, we hold. With soldiers it would be very doubtful, for great forces could be brought to bear upon them—upon us only forts.*

Having disposed of Walker and Beauregard, the navy would not allow any other such forts to crop up.

Du Pont seems not to have been overly worried about an attack from the Mosquito Fleet or the army's role as spectator. With the conference completed, he invited Captain Lardner aboard the *Wabash* to dine with him. Lardner did not come alone; he brought an unusual guest, a contraband from the

Author's collection.

Where Hilton Head and Low Bay Point Defied

Charleston area who had defected to his ship. This contraband was viewed by Du Pont as "a very intelligent one." Recently departed from slavery in that city, this unnamed contraband provided the following intelligence: some companies had been rushed to Port Royal from Charleston, and General Ripley, an Ohioan gone South in command of South Carolina, was fortifying.

On November 5, the *Wabash* entered the harbor. Du Pont wrote to his wife, "Precious Sophie, we are inside, a great nautical feat, to have got this ship in." Apparently unaware of how much they outnumbered the Confederates, he went on: "If it pleases God to give us equal success in dealing with our enemies and their batteries, we shall attain our ends."

BROTHER AGAINST BROTHER

"Brother against brother" is a phrase often used when describing the Civil War. It was no mere expression—ties to country in that divisive conflict often pitted families against one another. In some cases, it was a polite feud or a battle fought with heated words or letters. Tragically, family members often faced one another on the same field of battle. One such incident occurred at the Battle of Port Royal between Percival and Thomas Drayton. The two brothers were scions of the venerable Drayton family of South Carolina. Their father was William Drayton, a prominent lawyer and politician who had relocated the family to Philadelphia in 1833.

Captain Percival Drayton, United States Navy. *Author's collection.*

Percival's ambition lay at sea. As a teenager, he entered the navy as a midshipman to learn the basic rudiments of life aboard a ship. As he advanced through the ranks, he traveled the globe in the company of the Brazilian, Mediterranean and Pacific naval squadrons. Percival made a hard choice when the Civil War erupted. He opted for the Union, a decision that placed him squarely against his elder brother, Thomas. As a commander, Percival was placed aboard the Pocahontas, *part of Du Pont's expedition. Some doubted his loyalty because of his Southern ties, but Du Pont had no such qualms. Percival's performance at the Battle of Port Royal, against the forces commanded by his brother, earned him promotion to captain.*

The Battle of Port Royal

> *He was transferred to a new ship, one of the new metal-plated monitor class ships, the* Passaic. *Percival was promoted to the position of flag captain under Rear Admiral Farragut. It was while serving with Farragut during the 1865 Battle of Mobile Bay that he became an unintentional element of a famous catchphrase. Mobile Bay was laced with mines, then called torpedoes. Seeing his ships hesitating, Farrugut barked, "Damn the torpedoes! Four bells! Captain Drayton, go ahead! Joucett, full speed!" This phrase is often condensed to "Damn the torpedoes! Full steam ahead!"*
>
> *Percival enjoyed a reputation as a patriot in the North after the war. He served as chief of the Bureau of Navigation. South Carolina never forgot the insult, however. The South Carolina General Assembly passed a formal condemnation of Percival and forbade him residency in his native state. Percival attempted to aid his brother financially after the war in order to regain control of family property. Percival died of illness in 1865, ending any hope of reconciliation.*
>
> *The older Thomas Drayton's calling was in a different branch of the military. He attended the United States Military Academy; one of his classmates was the future president of the Confederacy, Jefferson Davis. The two men remained lifelong friends. Thomas put his education to use in the Army Corps of Engineers and then, later, in the South Carolina Militia. Thomas severed his ties to the Federal army and contacted his old friend Davis to offer his service to the Confederacy. He was conferred the rank of brigadier general; his department was the Port Royal region.*
>
> *Few faulted Thomas for the loss at Port Royal. He was an able general who did his duty, but he was simply overwhelmed by the superior numbers of Federals. In 1862, he commanded infantry in General Lee's Army of Northern Virginia, surviving such battles as Second Manassas and Antietam. In these engagements, his competency was called into question. To silence his opponents, Thomas was shipped out to the western theater. Following the war, Thomas sold insurance and moved to several states, but he eventually returned to South Carolina, where he died in 1891.*

The *Vandalia*, a creaky ship built in 1828 and recently recommissioned, arrived inside the bar, summoned from the blockade around Savannah just as the *Susquehanna* had been drawn from its duties around Charleston. The *Unadilla* came in, as did Charles Steedman, a South Carolina man loyal to the Union, and his steamer, the *Bienville*. The other South Carolina captain who had professed loyalty to the Union, Percival Drayton, and his ship, the *Pocahontas*, had not been seen since the storm. Percival's brother, Thomas Fenwick Drayton, had a plantation—Fish Haul—on Hilton Head, and he served as the Confederate commander of Fort Walker. Gossips may have speculated about Percival's loyalties based on his family ties, but Du Pont knew this officer and knew that he would arrive as soon as possible.

Where Hilton Head and Low Bay Point Defied

On the fifth, Du Pont wanted to attack. He sent the *Mercury* and a couple of swifter ships to develop the batteries. They could faintly make out where Forts Walker and Beauregard were on the adjacent islands but lacked an idea of what sort of guns they could bring to bear on them. The reconnaissance, it was hoped, would bait the Confederate gunners into revealing their locations.

Bradley Sillick Osbon, a reporter who had accompanied the expedition, took part in this venture:

> On the morning of the 5th a slight scrimmage with Tattnall occurred, but nothing of any consequence. It was decided now to send in the Mercury, a small beam-engine steamer, to draw the fire of the forts, in order that we might calculate the number, class, and calibre of the enemy's guns. I went aboard the little vessel, as did Generals Sherman, Stevens, and Viele, and some of the other officers. There

FORT WALKER

On May 16, 1861, General P.G.T. Beauregard, then commander of the department in which South Carolina belonged, submitted the following report:

> I am of the opinion that the entrance to the magnificent and important harbor Port Royal can be effectually protected by two strong works on Hilton Head and Bay Point, on each side of the entrance, and a steel-clad, floating battery moored half way between the two, all armed with the heaviest rifled guns that can be made, but the construction not being practicable at present, I have resorted to local works.

Not long after this report was filed, Major Francis D. Lee received direct orders from General Beauregard to construct defensive works on the South Carolina coast. Beauregard, the hero of Fort Sumter, was himself an engineer of some merit and forwarded to Lee the general location where he desired the defenses to be placed, as well as the type and quantity of armaments required. Although the defenses were still in the planning phase, Robert Barnwell Rhett of the Charleston Mercury felt safe enough to proclaim, "The noble harbor of Port Royal is at last fully defended." He assured his readers that "any demonstration of the enemy in that neighborhood [is] rather a hopeless experiment."

In June 1861, Lee received a $15,000 appropriation for this military project. Early the next month, he organized a "party of artisans: in Charleston and brought

The Battle of Port Royal

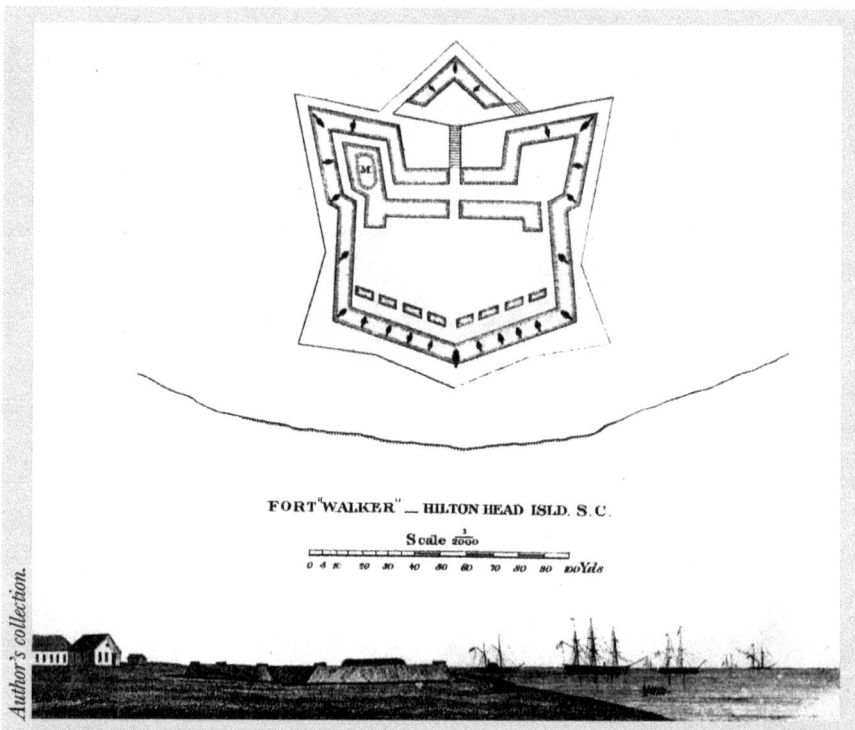

them to the work site." There was only one problem: there was no one available to build the fort. The local planters were to supply the workforce, meaning they were to lend their slaves to Lee to use as laborers. A bureaucratic oversight had left Lee without the authority he needed to impress the slaves, and the planters were unwilling to hand over their property. For three weeks, Lee and his artisans spent their time designing Fort Walker. When the order permitting him to impress the slaves into service finally arrived, he had created a masterpiece of military science. It was named in honor of the first Confederate secretary of war, LeRoy Pope Walker (an Alabama politician who thought the war would be a quick affair and, in a speech, offered to sop up all the blood spilled with his handkerchief).

Alfred Roman, Beauregard's official commissioned biographer, claimed in the general's biography that, originally, Beauregard had been against putting works at the entrance of Port Royal Harbor. According to Roman, Beauregard wanted smaller works in the inner harbor to protect the Charleston and Savannah Railroad approaches. Only after being pressed by Governor Pickens, Roman claims, did Beauregard lay out a design for the harbor forts. Beauregard's designs for Port Royal were far beyond the means of South Carolina, and Lee had to make the most with what little he had.

Lee did not just design the fort and depart; rather, he took part in the November 7 struggle. According to one officer's report, "Major F.D. Lee, South Carolina Engineers

Where Hilton Head and Low Bay Point Defied

and constructing engineer of Fort Walker, not only fought gallantly at the batteries, but afforded valuable assistance at other points during the contest."

After the Confederate evacuation, the incoming Federals left precise accounts of the fort:

> Fort Walker was found to be a regularly constructed enclosed bastioned work, with two water fronts, and an outwork in the rear commanding the approach by land. These defences mounted altogether twenty-three guns, all left in good condition and serviceable, among which were twelve 32-pounders, two 8 and 10-inch columbiads, two 6-inch rifled guns, several heavy sea-coast howitzers, and an English siege gun. A profusion of ammunition was left when the fort was abandoned. Fort Beauregard proved to be an enclosed work with four faces, each looking on the water, and mounting thirteen guns, including five 32s, and two 8 and 10-inch columbiads. Upon each flank of the main works, at a distance of about a hundred and fifty yards were smaller works, mounting two 24 and three 32-pounders, making in all twenty guns. In both Forts Walker and Beauregard there were furnaces for heating shot.

The invaders also penned glowing descriptions of Fort Walker. General T.W. Sherman referred to Walker as "the beautifully constructed works." Army officer Stephen Minot Weld said, "The fort was a very strong one and not much damaged by our fire." Viele noted that "the two works...were in themselves models in their construction; admirably designed." Upon seeing the fort up close, Du Pont himself remarked, "The works are most scientifically constructed and there is nothing like 'Walker' on the Potomac."

In the aftermath of the battle, the damage to Fort Walker was repaired and the structure improved. It was renamed Fort Welles in honor of the secretary of the Union navy, Gideon Welles. Today, the site of the fort is between two large beachfront homes in a gated community and is inaccessible unless arrangements are made with a sanctioned local tour company.

was no reticence on the part of the enemy as to exposing their strength. They let go at us with a will, the shot falling about us merrily. As each gun was fired I called its class and calibre, and General Sherman, who stood near me, said:

"How can you be sure of the size of those shot at this distance?"

"I am not sure," I said, "but I am used to measuring objects at sea with my eye, and I judge the calibre from the ring of smoke that forms the instant the gun is fired."

The Battle of Port Royal

Fort Beauregard

The construction of Fort Beauregard was supervised by Captain J.W. Gregory (also spelled Gregorie). It was named in honor of General P.G.T. Beauregard. There is far less documentation on Beauregard's construction, but it can be safely surmised that the growth of this log-and-earth fort mirrored that of its bigger sister, Walker, across the harbor. A Federal report gives the following details:

> Report of Acting Lieutenant Barnes, U.S. Navy, giving inventory of guns and munitions of war contained in Fort Beauregard.
>
> U. S. Steam Frigate Wabash,
> Port Royal, S.C., November ft, 1861.
> Sir: In compliance with your order of yesterday, I have this day visited the fort known as Fort Beauregard, situated upon Bay Point, and there instituted a careful survey of the ordnance and

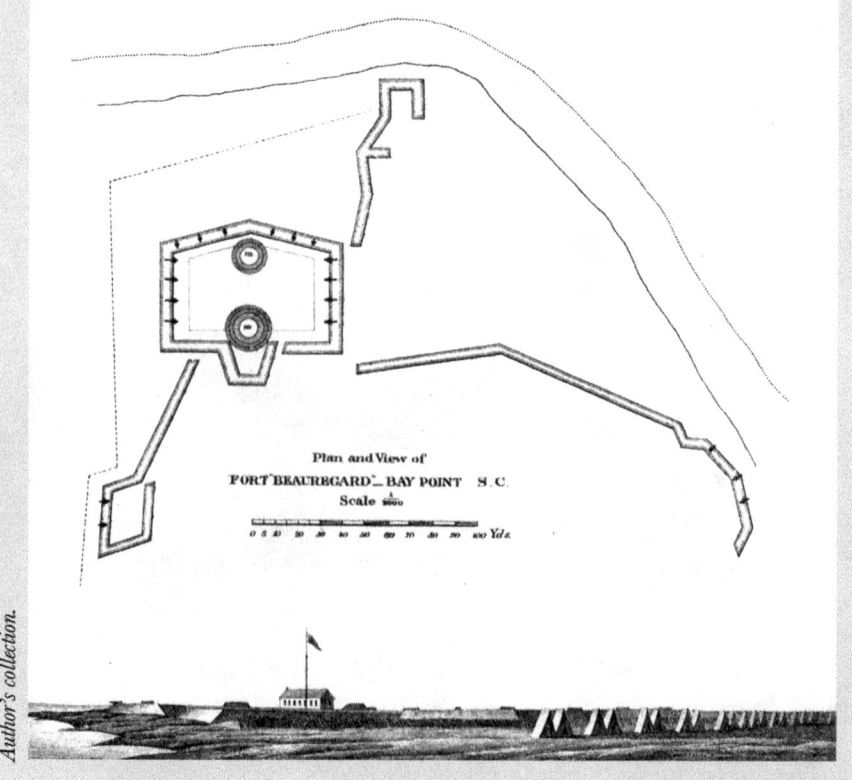

Author's collection.

Where Hilton Head and Low Bay Point Defied

ammunition contained in and lying about the fort, and have to report as follows:

The fort has four faces, upon which guns are mounted, each face looking on the water and each gun so mounted as to command the water approach to Broad and Beaufort rivers. The guns are thirteen in number, of the following sizes:

Five 32's, navy pattern, 1845; all in good order.

One rifled 6-inch, new, marked C.S.A., 1861; J.R.A. & Co., T.F.; gun burst and carriage destroyed.

Five seacoast guns, 42-pounders, long and very heavy; all in good order.

One 10-inch columbiad, marked C.S.A., 1861; J.R.A. & Co., T.F.; Palmetto coat of arms; weight 13,226 pounds; spiked with steel spike and loaded.

One 8-inch columbiad; same marks as the 10-inch; in good order.

There is also upon each flank of the main work, at a distance of about 150 yards from it, a small work built to command the land approach along the beach, as well as the channel abreast. These outer works are connected by earthworks with the main fort.

Upon the outer work on the left flank are mounted 2 24-pounders, in good order, marked S.C. Upon the outer work on the right flank are mounted 3 32-pounders, 63-hundred weight, navy pattern, 1845; all in good order.

Within the fort were also 2 field pieces pounders, 6-pounders, old Spanish pattern; making in all 20 pieces of ordnance of the classes as above enumerated.

Within the fort I found a great amount of ammunition

> scattered about in disorder. In the shell room were several hundred shells filled and fuzed for the various sizes of guns. The magazine is filled with powder, put up in cylinders ready for use; the powder appears to be of most excellent quality. There are two furnaces for heating shot, both filled with shot, some of them partly melted. The ammunition chests are nearly all full of powder. In a pool of water in the rear large quantities of ammunition are lying where it was thrown by the enemy before retreating.
> I am, very respectfully, your obedient servant,
> John S. Barnes,
> Acting Lieutenant.

> *It may interest the reader to know that later, when we landed, my tally was found to be correct.*
>
> *We were under fire in the little* Mercury *for the better part of an hour, and while some of the missiles passed uncomfortably close, we came out unharmed, having acquired full information as to the enemy's armament; also, on my part, some notes for my paper and some crude sketches, which I made for* Harper's Weekly. *We now reported to the flagship and a general council of war was held. A chart was spread upon the table and everything was prepared to call the meeting to order, when I rose to leave the cabin. The Flag Officer checked me.*
>
> *"Where are you going, Mr. Osbon?" he asked.*
>
> *I said, "It has occurred to me that this is not the place for a newspaper man."*

John Rodgers, also onboard the *Mercury*, later wrote:

> *It was beautiful firing on both sides—we put a number of 11 inch shells into their camp and a number of their shot fell so near that once could scarcely have put a knife between the vessels and the shot. Some of the rigging was cut—I found the excitement not unpleasant, and when a shot splashed up close I involuntarily exclaimed "well done rebel."*

With the intelligence collated, Du Pont stated, "Everything was ready and the fleet of twelve vessels in all were organized and given their stations." The *Wabash* and the *Susquehanna* came too near the *Fishing Rip* shoal and were grounded, stalling the attack. The buoys were up, but they were strangers inside Port Royal Sound; navigation was still touch-and-go in places.

Where Hilton Head and Low Bay Point Defied

Du Pont lamented, "We have done an immense day's work in getting in and preparing the ship for action…but I feel I acted wisely."

Even more serious was the benefit this delay would give to the Confederates. There was now time for additional reinforcements to arrive and to further fortify their positions.

Wednesday, November 6, found the navy still at anchor and the solders still penned in cramped holds. William Thompson Lusk recorded the seething impatience felt by these men. They had arrived at their destination, but

> *that Navy though is a slow affair and we abused it mightily, being impatient to decide the fate of the expedition. Our naval commanders Commodore Du Pont and Secretary of Navy Wells received the most unflattering notices. Why would they not begin?*

Du Pont explained, "It is blowing fresh from the SW, and the tide compels us to delay our departure to attack the forts. I shall wait for the tide but possibly move in spite of the wind."

The *Ericsson*, another of the troublesome transports, had problems with its new surroundings. It was grounded and "would have went to pieces," Du Pont claimed, if he had not sent the *R.B. Forbes* to the rescue.

Near sunset, a trio of army officers came to see Du Pont. He braced himself for the questions and polite accusations. To his surprise, Sherman and his fellow officers had come to tell him that they fully supported his decision and were glad they had waited. Du Pont's aide, Davis, summed up the general feeling of those in command of the expedition: "Wise councils prevailed, and we postponed the attack till the next day."

Du Pont was disappointed about the aborted attack; nevertheless, his letter to Sophie had an optimistic tone: "We are holding the roadstead like Hampton Roads, and the show of ships is very striking, and if we had set out to take a great harbor in the flank of the enemy, we have it already."

November 7, weather permitting, would be the day of the attack.

CHAPTER 6

IRON TEMPEST IN INCESSANT BLAST

The position was deemed a strong one, because it seemed that any attacking fleet which should attempt to pass those jaws of iron would surely be broken up and destroyed, and to endeavor to take both by assault without a protracted siege seemed even more dangerous.
—a reporter commenting on Fort Walker and Fort Beauregard

Charles Davis awoke on Thursday morning, November 7, in his bunk in the tiny cabin he shared with several other officers aboard the *Wabash*. His sleeping mind must have been working beneath the surface on the plans they had discussed late into the evening because he had scarcely opened his eyes when he was struck by an idea. Without stopping to dress in his uniform, he hurried down the narrow hall to Du Pont's stateroom.

Had the *Wabash* and *Susquehanna* not been grounded on Tuesday, November 5, the plan for capturing the sound would have been to take the forts singly. Valuable intelligence had been gathered by their reconnaissance passing the forts. They had roughly determined the quantity and type of guns mounted in the forts, as well as their general construction. The biggest threat—Fort Walker, bearing the most guns—was to be reduced first. They would approach and annihilate the resistance it offered, without coming under any serious fire from Fort Beauregard. The distance between the two forts across the sound was 2.2 miles, an extreme range for supporting fire. Fort Beauregard's cannons would be hard-pressed to have any impact on their operations against the isolated Walker.

Iron Tempest in Incessant Blast

A more succinct summary of the basic principle of the attack was given by Davis:

> *Du Pont and the two Rodgerses, and myself agreed entirely that the best method of fighting in a heavy-armed ship like this, throwing shells almost exclusively, with a really formidable battery, was to come simply to the point, and to depend upon the destructive agency, and the terror inspired by it, of a shower of iron hail, or iron hell, dropped in the briefest time in one spot.*

Davis's sudden inspiration was a modification of this plan:

> *It occurred to me that the direct approach to Fort Walker* [Hilton Head] *had the advantage of avoiding the fire of Beauregard* [Bay Point], *leaving us to reserve all our force and fire for the former—an advantage I had perhaps thought too much of—yet that I had overlooked another advantage upon reflection, I felt convinced ought not to be thrown away; and that was the advantage arising from making an approach to Fort Walker from the north, on which side we could enfilade the water-faces of the battery, and encounter the fort at the beginning, on its weakest flank.*

The only downside to this plan was that the ships in the attack would first have to pass Fort Beauregard "and begin the day with an unnecessary engagement that would contribute nothing to the main object of the day's work."

Essentially, the *Wabash* would lead two parallel columns of ships into the sound to the midway point between the two forts. Once past the forts, the five gunboats in the starboard column would break off. Commodore Tattnall's Mosquito Fleet was not forgotten. Like its namesake, it was a nuisance that needed to be swatted. These five gunboats were to act as a protective screen against the Confederate navy's forays into the battle.

The other ships, without stopping, would keep sailing at a pace of about six miles an hour and would swing down to fire on Walker. The intelligence they gathered showed that Fort Walker's water face, the structure of the fort pointed away from the harbor, was weaker than the other sides. Taking in the flank was a concept military men of all ages knew the value of. Firing at this angle also opened the fort to enfilading, meaning that the ships' cannons could fire unobstructed down the full length of the fort, causing immeasurable peril to those Confederates who tried to work the guns on the ramparts. This design flaw would prove to be Walker's Achilles' heel. The Federals would exploit this weakness to the fullest with this new system and be able to take shots at both forts in the process.

The Battle of Port Royal

The opening gun of the Battle of Port Royal. *Author's collection.*

After pounding Walker, they would circle back again to hit Beauregard on the other end of the sound, and then get another crack at Walker on the way down. They would continue turning and firing in this two-mile ellipse, trading blows with the two forts until something gave.

The tradeoff of this plan was that it was unlikely that they would be much more in Fort Beauregard's range as they turned. In their book *History of Beaufort, 1514–1861*, authors Lawrence S. Rowland, Alexander Moore and George C. Rogers made the following insightful observation about the plan:

> *The brilliance of the maneuver was that each ship in Du Pont's fleet would be under the guns of the forts for a few minutes at a time, while the fixed fortifications were continuously under fire from the naval guns.*

Du Pont recognized the improvement. Davis's modifications were sent out to the captains of the ships that were going to be part of the engagement. The two men went to breakfast. Following his meal, Du Pont returned to his cabin, closed the door and got down on his knees. At the end of his "earnest prayer," he read

Iron Tempest in Incessant Blast

a little more from his devotional and then glanced at the photo of his wife. He felt calm, ready for his duty, secure in the sense that the "eye of a merciful father" was upon him. He strode out of his room and began the attack.

***

It was November 4, a Monday. General Thomas Fenwick Drayton was in his headquarters in Beaufort when he got the news. Their fears had been realized—the fleet had come, flying the banner of war, to South Carolina. According to the report of Colonel William C. Heyward, thirty or more ships had assembled off the entrance to Port Royal and more were expected. Leaving Beaufort in a steamer, Drayton made his way to Bay Point. It was late afternoon by the time he drew close to the fort. On the way in, he had passed Tattnall's Mosquito Fleet, watching off to the side, waiting to test its mettle again against its far-superior Federal counterpart.

Drayton disembarked. The commander of Fort Beauregard, Colonel R.G.M. Dunovant, came out to meet him. The officers remained in deep consultation for the next six and a half hours, closing the meeting at 1:30 a.m. Drayton's day was not over yet. He boarded the steamer again and went out to speak with Commodore Tattnall. The two discussed their views at length aboard the

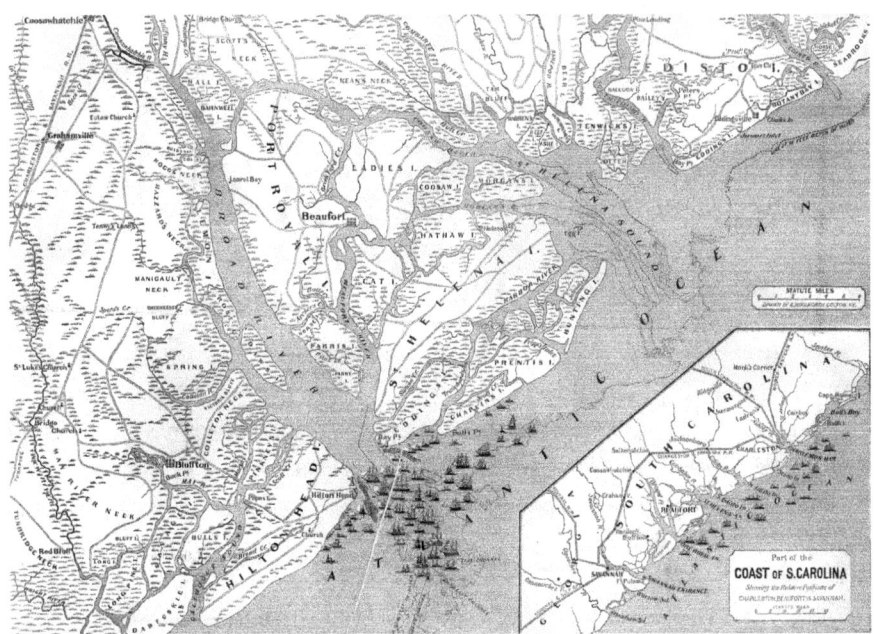

A map showing the Federal fleet massing for the November 7, 1861 attack. *Author's collection.*

THE BATTLE OF PORT ROYAL

The interior of Fort Walker, circa 1865. *Library of Congress.*

flagship. Weary but determined, Drayton pushed on. He bade farewell to the navy contingent, boarded the steamer and was transported over to Fort Walker at Hilton Head. It was daylight when he reached solid ground again.

Drayton's first action was to dispatch a mounted courier, carrying orders to bring Captain Stuart and the Ninth Regiment to reinforce the gunners in Walker. Instead of sleeping, Drayton conducted a thorough inspection of the fort:

> *On inspecting Fort Walker shortly after my arrival I found twenty guns, of various caliber, mounted upon the ramparts, thirteen of which were on the channel battery, viz, one 10-inch columbiad in the center, flanked to the right by five 32-pounders and one 9-inch Dahlgren rifled cannon, and to the left by six other cannon in the following order: One 32-pounder, one 8-inch columbiad, three 42-pounders, and one rifled 24-pounder; north bastion, one 32-pounder; south bastion, one 32-pounder, one 8-inch howitzer, and one long 12-pounder; south flank of bastion, one navy 32-pounder; demi-lune, two 24-pounders; redan, one navy 8-inch howitzer. Of these eight guns one in the north bastion and two in the south flank could occasionally be used against the ships of war. The rest were for the land defense. To man the guns within the fort and for an infantry reserve outside we had, until re-enforcements came from Savannah on*

Iron Tempest in Incessant Blast

> *the afternoon of the 6th, two companies of Colonel Wagener's First Regiment Artillery, South Carolina Militia, numbering 152 men; three companies of Colonel Heyward's Ninth* [Eleventh] *Regiment South Carolina Volunteers, 210 men; four companies of Col. R.G.M. Dunovant's Twelfth Regiment South Carolina Volunteers, under Major Jones, 260 men. Total, 622 men. There were stationed on the beach at Camp Lookout, 6 miles off, Capt. I.H. Screvens Mounted Guerrillas, numbering 65, who acted as scouts and couriers.*

Drayton also got his first look with his own eyes at his enemy. Langdon Cheves, one of his aides, remarked:

> *As soon as I got on the Island on Wednesday evening the first thing that struck my eye was the great fleet which had been lying motionless for days in such street like lines that our camp called it the city of Lincolnton.*

The sheer size of the fleet struck one Confederate defender as ludicrous. He called it "gigantic preparations" and "enormous expenditures—the outfit of nothing less than an immense armada to rout a handful of men from their sand holes in the beach."

Drayton was still awake at 9:00 a.m. when Tattnall again gallantly steamed out to exchange shots with the sounding parties of the fleet. There was little these boats could do besides make a quick feint and then retreat behind the forts. Several of the fleet followed. In his official report, General Drayton wrote that they "engaged both batteries for about forty-five minutes, with no other injury than 3 men slightly burned in Fort Beauregard from the explosion of a caisson struck by a rifle shell."

Drayton turned in when the excitement died down to grab what rest he could. The odds were very clearly stacked in the favor of the Federals, and this was clear for all to see. Still, many of the Confederates were optimistic.

Robert Chisolm had acquired quite a taste for a liquid beverage that one of the surgeons he served under called a "prophylactic." This drink was said to cure the sick and make the well feel even better. It also had, according to Chisolm, "the further effect of belittling the strength of the enemy and increasing our own." Possibly while imbibing, he wandered the camp of tents that had cropped up behind Walker:

> *On land, during that night, the best glee-songs were sung, and tales told around the camp-fires. This is always the case before a battle; when about to leave this world, we would recall the pleasant happy times in it.*

The Battle of Port Royal

Slaves and Freedmen

Colonel Thomas Wentworth Higginson and Lieutenant Colonel Trowbridge, Federal officers stationed in the Beaufort area after the Battle of Port Royal, had intimate contact with former slaves. They learned from conversation that a spiritual, "Many Thousand Go," despite an antislavery message, was sung during the hard forced labor of Fort Walker's construction.

> No more peck o' corn for me,
> No more, no more—
> No more peck o' corn for me,
> Many tousand go.
> No more driver's lash for me, *[Twice]*
> No more, &c.
> No more pint o' salt for me, *[Twice]*
> No more, &c.
> No more hundred lash for me, *[Twice]*
> No more, &c.
> No more mistress' call for me,
> No more, No more—
> No more mistress' call for me,
> Many tousand go.

Popular historian Benjamin Lossing wrote:

> Most of the slaves remained. They refused to follow their masters. Groups of them actually stood upon the shore with little bundles containing their worldly possessions, ready to go board the ships of the invaders, who, they had been told, were coming to steal or sell the negroes in Cuba, or to kill and bury them in the Sound.

A more boastful Confederate wrote:

> *We will give shell two to one, and hot and cold shot in quantities to suit. We are all ready for them, and will give good account of ourselves to the Yankees. I will write you next week, and give you an account of the fight, the number of prisoners, and the lists of the vessels destroyed.*

Iron Tempest in Incessant Blast

Drayton was back on the scene the next day. Forty-five sails were counted in the water, yet there were still more to come, he had been informed. The big ship must be the *Wabash*, swarmed by its lesser children—the gunboats, transports and assorted steamers. Some of the boats were nothing more than coal barges, floating refueling stations that had come brazenly into the harbor to refuel the cargo holds of the fighting ships.

In the evening, the ships started to move. The gunships pulled forward, the ancillary ships shifted away—every sign pointed to imminent attack. Drayton wasn't too concerned about the hammer following on the sixth—the "weather was very boisterous." He was sure that they wanted to get their attack underway but also knew that they were good enough sailors to not attempt an attack or landing while the tides and winds were high.

This gave time for reinforcements to come in. At four o'clock, loud cheers erupted from the throats of his men. It wasn't the Ninth, like he had requested by courier, but the first Georgia men to arrive. Approximately 150 Georgians under Captain Berry came to take part in the defense; also arriving was Captain Read's battery, which would add two twelve-pound howitzers and 50 men to the fray.

Two hours after the Georgia men had arrived and been put into position, news came that Colonel Desaussure and the Fifteenth South Carolina were at hand. They were disembarking at Seabrook's Wharf near Skull Creek. Soon, 650 more men would bolster their defense.

Night fell, and although it wasn't out of the question, a night attack was highly unlikely. They were able to relax a little more. Robert Chisolm recalled that he heard "soft sounds of music over the water"; the shipboard bands were playing and "the crossing of lights in the fleet showed us plainly that the attack was to be made in the morning."

✷✷✷

Almost every account of the Battle of Port Royal makes mention of the flawless weather of that Thursday. Chisolm noted:

> *The morning of that November Thursday was perfect. The sun rose with unusual splendor in a cloudless sky; no breath of wind marred the smooth surface of the ocean, and it shone like a thousand mirrors. It was a day when a man forgets he exists.*

The *Charleston Mercury* proclaimed bitterly, "The day was beautiful—calm and clear, with scarcely a cloud in the heavens—just such a day as our invaders would have ordained, if they could, to carry on operations." T.F. Drayton stated, "At last the memorable 7th dawned upon us bright and serene, not a ripple upon the broad expanse of water to disturb the accuracy of that magnificent armada." John A. Wagener wrote:

> *The enemy had chosen a day which was entirely propitious to him. The water was as smooth as glass. The air was just sufficient to blow the smoke of his guns into our faces, where it would meet the column of our own smoke and prevent our sight, except by glimpses.*

Colonel R.G.M. Dunovant of the Twelfth South Carolina noted that "the wind lulled and the water was unusually smooth."

One of Du Pont's many biographers captures the pre-battle preparations onboard the ships:

> *Tars sanded down the decks…put out the fired, and rigged the pumps; barefoot powder monkeys lugged ammunition to the guns, surgeons spread out their instruments; old salts eyed the Confederate forts, rolling up their sleeves to "give them Hatteras."*

In the wake of the departing gunships, the transports and the multitude of smaller craft nestled near their hulls, bobbing up and down almost in expectation. Should the navy be unable to dislodge the Confederates, the men in these tiny boats would have to storm the beaches at the forts at the end of a musket. Considering the army ships carrying most of their ammunition and field guns had not arrived, this was an undesirable option. Captain Hazard Stevens wrote of this secondary component of the attack, stating that the soldiers were to "land in small boats on the open beach during the naval bombardment and carry the works by assault, in case the navy failed to shell the enemy out."

Accordingly, on the morning of November 7, the surfboats and all other boats belonging to the vessels were launched and brought alongside or astern of the transports. The troops of Steven's and Wright's brigades were provided with ammunition and one day's cooked rations and held in readiness to land and attack. While they awaited this movement, the following order was written by General Stevens and read to them:

> *Headquarters, Second Brigade, Expeditionary Corps*
> *S.S.* Vanderbilt, *November 7, 1861*

Iron Tempest in Incessant Blast

STEPHEN ELLIOTT, JR.

Author's collection.

General Orders No. 5

The brigadier general commanding the second brigade trustfully appeals to each man of his command this day to strike a signal blow for his country. She has been stabbed by traitorous hands and by her favored sons. Show by your acts that the hero age has not passed away and that patriotism still lives. Better to fall nobly in the forlorn hope of vindication of home and nationality than to live witness of the triumph of sacrilegious cause. The Lord God of battles will direct us; to Him let us humbly appeal this day to vouchsafe to us his crowning mercy; and may those of us who survive, when the evening sun goes down ascribe to Him, and not to ourselves, the glorious victory.

Those soldiers who were not being prepped for the beach attack stayed on the transports as spectators. As can be imagined, all eyes were on the fleet.

Every vessel of the fleet of transports was alive with soldiers watching the movements. The boys not satisfied with the ships view from the deck, climbed into the rigging of the ships for a better view, on to and into every available

The Battle of Port Royal

Author's collection.

> spot, from bow-sprit to paddle-box, up to the masthead, like a swarm of bees...was there ever such an audience watching such a drama?

Another soldier from New Hampshire was struck by the appearance of the flagship:

> The Wabash had a peculiar appearance that morning, to those of us that had never seen a naval fight. The boys said she had her "sleeves rolled up." All the extra spars, yards, topmasts, etc. had been taken in, and in some respects she looked like a partially dismantled ship. She was simply gotten ready for action.

Anticipation was just as high on the Confederate side. Chisolm left the fort's hospital, the surgeons carefully laying out their grim instruments of salvation—the bone saws, hooks and clamps—on operating tables. As a volunteer, he had the freedom to move from his post into another. The next view he described could have come only from the ramparts:

> One by one the big black men-of-war drifted out of the crowds slightly inland for about a mile, when, at a blast from the flagship, method grew out of disorder. Speed was increased and flags hoisted as each ship fell into her place in the line of battle as they approached the battery. On the line came, the flagship leading, men in the

Iron Tempest in Incessant Blast

The Battle of Port Royal, November 7, 1861.

> *topmast...the hulls looming up black out of the clear water, flying flags of every color, shape, and size no smoke. They did not seem to be a separate thing, but each ship part of one whole...Flags carried his* [Du Pont's] *orders, and flags returned the answer. It did not look like war; it was a picture—a glorious pageant.*

German-born Colonel John A. Wagener noticed that the fleet had begun to move. His instincts told him that this was the beginning. He ordered the long roll sounded; the sustained beating was a call to his men that attack was imminent and to prepare themselves. In his official report, he notes proudly that "in one and a half minutes every cannoneer was at his post." He also noted that the "the sailing vessels of our opponents were towed by his steamers, and thus could maneuver on the broad expanse of Port Royal with the accuracy of well-trained battalions."

General Drayton observed the fleet "advancing in battle array to vomit forth its iron hail with all the spiteful energy of long-suppressed rage and conscious strength."

It was 8:00 a.m. when Du Pont gave the order to move. The main column consisted of the *Wabash, Susquehanna, Mohican, Seminole, Pawnee, Unadilla, Ottawa, Pembina* and *Vandalia*, towed by the *Isaac Smith*, which had lost all but one of its guns in the storm. The flanking column was made up of the ships *Bienville*, Captain Ammen's *Seneca*, the *Curlew*, the *Penguin* and the *Augusta*. Thirty minutes

Author's collection.

later, the *Wabash* was headed toward the fort. At 9:00 a.m., the signal flags relayed the command for close order.

"Opening the Ball" was a term that was popular in the nineteenth century. It appears over and over again in Civil War–era literature and battle reports as slang for the start of a battle. The Battle of Port Royal was no exception. A *New York Times* correspondent wrote, "The ball opened…and a warm ball it was." The exact time of the first shot varied from observer to observer; the most trustworthy accounts "start the ball" at either 9:25 or 9:26 a.m.

The lanyard was pulled on a nine-inch Dahlgren gun inside Fort Walker. A defective fuse exploded the shell near the muzzle of the barrel—an inauspicious beginning and an unfortunate omen for the defenders. Weld, in one of the transports, marked the commencement: "When we were about six miles from the land we saw the white smoke curling up in the air from a point on the left of the sound called Hilton Head. This was followed by the heavy 'boom' of the report." Fort Beauregard fired a shot almost immediately afterward. The soldiers in the transports cheered, perhaps in admiration of their foes' bravery; perhaps it was just a release of pent-up anxiety. There was a lull. The ships had not yet returned fire. A reporter for *Harper's Weekly* scribbled, "But no firing from our side yet."

The *Wabash*, which some of the Confederates had misidentified as the *Minnesota*, a ship still in Virginia, discharged its opening salvo. The *Harper's* reporter recounted:

> *In a few minutes the* Wabash *opened a smart fire, throwing her shells into the woods where the rebels were camped in some force. After firing a few guns to ascertain the range, she opened a broadside fire on both batteries, which was one of the finest sights witnessed in this country. Now the troops did cheer. It was both hearty and long.*

The *Susquehanna* was the next ship in range to fire a volley from its guns. The action quickly became general on land and water. A Connecticut man watching said, "Broadside after broadside were poured into those doomed works of treason."

Another reporter, fighting for space with the soldiers on the transports, penned the following description:

> *The air was filled with whizzing shells, which burst above and below the vessels, while little puffs of white smoke dotted the air, and little spurts of water marked where the shells dipped and sank.*

Before 11:30 a.m., the *Wabash* was less than 600 yards from Fort Walker. Its engine was drastically slowed; all of the ships in the attacking column followed similar orders. Du Pont explained:

> *When abreast of the fort the engine was to be slowed and the movement reduced to only as much as would be just sufficient to overcome the tide, to preserve the order of battle by passing the batteries in slow succession and to avoid becoming a fixed mark for the enemy's fire.*

Sighting its cannons at just 550 yards, the *Wabash* unleashed a lethal barrage.

John Rodgers, in a letter to a friend, dated November 9, 1861, Port Royal Harbor, and later published in the November 14 edition of the *New York Tribune*, called the *Wabash*

> *a destroying angel, hugging the shore, calling the soundings with cold indifference, allowing the engine only to give steerage way, signaling the vessels their various evolutions, and at the same time raining shells, as in target practice, too fast to count. During the action, I looked carefully at the fort with a powerful sky-glass. Shell fell in it as fast as a horse's feet beat the ground on a gallop.*

During the circuit, Davis commented on the fire of a large gun at Fort Beauregard:

> *If I had known the existence and position of that venomous rifled eighty-pounder on the salient of Fort Beauregard, to the fire of which we were exposed as we advanced, and, still more, if I had known the rapidity and accuracy with which it served, I should have indulged a little more reflection perhaps. Every shot from that pestilential devil which was, I imagine, directed by a navy officer (resigned) either struck us or went forty feet of the bridge on which Du Pont, the Rogerses (John and Raymond), the first lieutenant (Corbin), and myself were standing. It was evidently aimed, according to Southern custom, at the officers, and aimed, I have no doubt, by some one of our old brother officers turned rebel.*

Inside Fort Walker, Drayton despaired:

> *In spite of our fire, directed with deliberation and coolness, the fleet soon passed both batteries apparently unharmed, and then returning delivered in their changing rounds a terrific shower of shot and shell in flank and front.*

Already, the fort had lost some of its firepower—a thirty-two-pounder had been shattered very early in the engagement by a round shot from one of the Federal guns. It ran out of ammunition for a second three-pounder.

Defective or damaged components robbed the Confederates of even more weaponry. After the fourth fire, a ten-inch Columbiad bounded over the limber and became useless; the twenty-four-pounder rifled cannon was choked while ramming down a shell and lay idle during nearly the whole engagement. The shells for the nine-inch Dahlgren were also too large. The fourth shell attempted to be rammed home could not be driven all the way (it was discharged at great risk anyway). Colonel Heyward put it bluntly: "Many of our guns were disabled by them or rendered useless by various accidents."

Lack of proper equipment also hampered their efforts. Two forty-two-pounder carronades—small smoothbore cannons—arrived just before the fleet began its attack. The carronades were lacking carriages, however, and in order

Iron Tempest in Incessant Blast

to get some use out of them, Major Francis D. Lee recalled that these items were "simply buried in the sand to such depth and with such directions as to enable us to have at least one fire in the event of an attempt to storm the work."

Getting the guns to fire was only part of the struggle. Colonel Wagener commented on the difficulty of hitting their attackers:

> *No sooner did we obtain his range than it would be changed and time after time rechanged, while the deep water permitted him to choose his own position, and fire shot after shot and shell after shell with the precision of target practice.*

Handicapped, but not ineffectual, the Confederate gunners turned in an impressive performance. They managed to land several blows during the attack. The flagship was an attractive target. One shot smashed into the vessel, dismounting a gun, killing the captain of the gun crew and leaving three others wounded. A total of twenty injuries were reported on that ship alone. In his after-action report, C.R.P. Rodgers details the damage inflicted on the *Wabash*:

> *Her spars and hull were struck nine times. A shot from an 80-pounder rifled cannon passed directly through the center of the mainmast about 12 feet above the rail; another shot struck the forward part of the same mast, carrying away the forward chafing batten. We have two shots in the water line, one of which makes a leak in the after magazine passage. The spanker boom was shot away, as was also the starboard lower boom and spare maintopsail yard. The other shots struck the rail, the sides, and the deck. The mainmast is much injured, but I hope to secure it for good service. I attribute the safety of the ship to the short distance at which she engaged Fort Walker, the enemy's shot passing over us.*

The *Pocahontas* was shot through the mainmast and the boom topping lift, and several small pieces of rigging were cut away.

The *Seminole* was struck six times, once in the hull above the water line. Some of the crew received slight splinter wounds, but there were no fatalities.

The *Susquehanna*'s hull was hit ten times and in twenty different parts of the rigging. Two men were seriously wounded, one was killed and another was slightly injured.

Six shots hit the *Mohican*, leaving no casualties or serious damage.

Multiple shots struck the *Bienville*, one passing entirely through the ship. These hits killed one man and injured another three.

The *Unadilla* was far more fortunate; it suffered only six hits, leaving only minor damage.

The Battle of Port Royal

Bombardment of Forts Walker and Beauregard

By Isaac Mclellan

Written November 1861

Part I. The Arrival

I.

Six-and-sixty gallant ships, tempest-toss'd
By the angry seas assailed, well-nigh lost
Off hostile Carolina's sandy coast,
Spread the straining, daring sail;
They had come from Northern shores far away,
They had battled with old ocean's stormy spray,
But triumphant still their course southward lay
Through the equinoctial gale.

II.

Wild surges in mountainous billows rose,
Wild the gale its majestic trumpet blows,
Wild the night with intenser darkness grows,
As the buffeting, brave fleet,
Struggles on, staggers blindly through the gloom—
No light, save the lightning, to illume,
To warn them where the tumbling breakers boom,
Where the eddying whirlpools beat;

III.

But the perils of the deep 'scap'd at last,
With torn and tattered canvas on each mast,
Behold the noble navy sailing fast
By the headlands of the shore!
Like a flock of white-wing'd owl, see! they come;
Like the sea-birds to their nests struggling home,
When the tempests out at sea lash the foam,
And the ruffian surges roar.

Iron Tempest in Incessant Blast

IV.

When they anchored by those shores so serene,
What a bright—what a soft, delicious scene!
With hues of rose, and hues of living green,
Beamed upon the seamen's view!
Not a ripple, not a dimple crisp'd the deep;
So pellucid, that the coral groves that sleep
Far below, were disclosed in all their sweep, Gay with every prismy hue!

V.

Far along the curving shores gleam'd the sand;
High aloft the branching palms would expand,
And the orange and the lime o'er the land
Wav'd their globes of sparkling gold;
Like emeralds shine the grasses and the leaves;
The grape its fruit and foliage interweaves,
And the ripened Indian corn, with its sheaves,
Is in ruddy bloom unroll'd.

VI.

White as foam shone the cotton o'er the plain,
As if snows, and the sleety, icy rain,
Their flaky storm has showered forth again
From winter's frosty urn;
Soft, soft the odorous land-breeze seaward blows,
Delicious with magnolia and the rose,
And the spicy air so sweet as it flows,
When flowers their incense burn.

Part II. The Battle

VII.

'Twas a fair scene—a grand, enchanting view;
Yet o'er that land, from fort to fortress, flew
A traitor's banner, while a rebel crew
In arms each fortress holds.
Not there the brave, bright, starry flag might float,
Cast its broad shield o'er rampart and o'er moat,

The Battle of Port Royal

Nor Freedom's battery, from its iron throat,
Salute the spangled folds.

VIII.

Fair glanced the day along Port Royal's tide,
Glanced o'er embattled forts on either side,
Where Hilton Head and Low Bay Point defied
The armada of the free;
A martial show, that vast, invading fleet!
When rose their flag, when mustering-drums were beat;
When rang the cheer that all the shores repeat,
Re-echoing o'er the sea!

IX.

Black men-of-war, their decks array'd for fight;
Vast transports, glittering with battalions bright;
Gunboats and steamships—'twas a gallant sight—
A panorama grand!
Each ship, like wrestler, stripped to dare the fray;
The guns, full-shotted, rang'd in long array;
The crews, impatient for the battle-day,
A stern and stalwart band.

X.

Then came the conflict. From Fort Walker's wall
Glanced the red fires, fast sped the hissing ball;
Thick smokes, volcanic, hover'd like a pall,
A dim, sulphurous vail;
The Bay Point batteries, like a furnace, cast
Their iron tempest in incessant blast;
How might survive the crews, the spar, the mast,
Before that fearful hail!

XI.

Yet all in vain! The star-flag still arose,
Nailed to each mast, a target for its foes;
The rough tars cheer, and on each frigate goes
In undismay'd career;
Stern Dupont leads his **Wabash** *to the goal,*

Iron Tempest in Incessant Blast

And Pawnee, Susquehanna, Seminole,
And stout Bienville *their dread thunders roll,*
'Mid shout and battle-cheer.

XII.

Stern Dupont, in that tempest's very midst,
Through lurid flames, and the artillery's mist,
Where crash'd the ball, and hurtling bullets hiss'd,
The noble frigate led.
For three long, bloody hours, he stubborn stood
Environed by that fierce and fiery flood;
While blush'd his decks with bubbling, loyal blood,
With scuppers chok'd and red.

XIII.

Three times that triple dance he fearless led;
Three times that circuit, that ellipse so dread;
Three times, 'mid splintering spar and falling dead,
He led the merciless path;
Three times his frigates and his gunboats well
Replied with hot-shot and with bursting shell,
enfilading those walls, that quak'd and fell
Beneath the scorching wrath!

XIV.

Thick flew the shell within each rampart's breath;
High rose the brown sand in that storm of death;
So o'er the desert doth Sirocco's breath
The caravan betray;
For three long hours that hurricane of gore
Through stony embrasure and rampart tore;
Guns were dismantled, men in many a score
Were withering swept away.

XV.

In vain their toil! In vain the rebel strife;
No human courage might withstand, with life,
That storm, when every moment was so rife
With desolating scourge!

> They fled, they flew, their arms aside were thrown;
> No guns were spiked, no standards were pluck'd down,
> But, wild with terror, o'er the country strewn,
> Their frantic race they urge!
>
> XVI.
> So ends the strife. The victor's guns are mute;
> The shouting squadron their brave flag salute;
> The veteran sailor and the raw recruit
> Their deafening cheerings pour;
> Prone drops the flag from yonder rebel mast—
> Soon to the breeze the Union Stars are cast;
> Avenged is Sumter's humbled flag at last,
> On Carolina's shore!
>
> XVII.
> Flag of our hearts, our symbol and our trust,
> Though treason trample thy bright folds in dust,
> Though dark rebellion, vile ambition's lust,
> Conspire to tear thee down;
> Millions of loyal lips will thee caress;
> Millions of loyal hearts thy stars will bless,
> Millions of loyal arms will round thee press,
> To guard thy old renown!

Lieutenant Wyman recounted the damage done to the *Pawnee*:

> *The following are the damages sustained by this vessel in the engagement of yesterday, viz: One 42-pounder shot starboard quarter at water line; one 18 inches above; these two shot cut four of the frame timbers, passed through the wardroom, knocking down bulkhead and demolishing drawers and bureau of the second room, also sideboard in wardroom and iron safe, knocking in a panel in the opposite room and partly destroying the bureau. One of them struck the deck above, raising two planks, and passed through a panel into the masters room. One round shot passed through the launches chock on the starboard side, through the launch, breaking the spare topmast and out through the port bulwarks. One passed through starboard forward port, striking the chase of No. 1 gun, then upper sill of port and the cap square,*

Iron Tempest in Incessant Blast

> *breaking the trunnion of the starboard forward gun. One passed through the bulwarks 3 feet forward of starboard forward gun, tearing off large splinters, struck the coaming of fore hatch and fell. One port side, amidships, at water line-did not penetrate. One grazed foreyard and one cut the main topgallant yard rope. All the injuries to crew were made by splinters.*

Two men were killed and three injured by this wooden shrapnel.

A lucky shot from Fort Walker smashed the steam drum aboard the *Penguin*. This sprayed scalding steam over the deck and stalled the engine. According to the official report, "From the Bay Point battery struck a skylight on the quarter-deck and buried itself deeply into an oak bitt-head on the port side, after carrying away the tiller chain on that side." The *Augusta* took the disabled ship in tow, sustaining one hit in its hull for its good deed.

The *Ottawa* was bold in the fight, coming so close to Fort Walker that it was fired upon with muskets. On the approach, a thirty-two-pound shot struck in the port waist of the ship, injuring six men, one of whom would have to have his leg amputated from the wounds.

The *Isaac Smith*, towing the *Vandalia*, lost its fore gaff to a shell. It used its single remaining gun to great execution, firing thirty-one times.

At the completion of the first ellipse, everything was going as planned. None of the ships had been sunk, and their fire seemed to be having great effect. On the second circuit, everything fell apart.

The second column, the gunboats, steamed ahead to deflect the Mosquito Fleet and to get into position to cover the right flank of the attack against Fort Beauregard. Leading the pack was the swift *Bienville*. When the big ships began their run, the Mosquito Fleet wisely withdrew to a safe distance. Upon seeing the *Bienville* pull off, Tattnall thought that it was injured or found the fire of the forts too hot. When the gunboat made an aggressive movement toward his little squadron, he realized his error and withdrew up a shallow waterway called Skull Creek. Knowing that it was too large a draft to chase Tattnall into the creek, the *Bienville* decided to join the main column.

"Fog of war" is a phrase coined by military theorist Carl von Clausewitz (1780–1831). It was a relatively new way to describe a condition of warfare as old as the institution itself. On the march or on the battlefield, unplanned-for actions and unforeseen conditions have a way of disrupting the best-laid plans. The fog of war descended on Du Pont during the bombardment, brought on by the unexpected behavior of his subordinates. Steedman, thinking that the Mosquito Fleet was pinned and no longer a concern, decided to add his boat to the attack on the forts. This set off a bizarre chain reaction.

The Battle of Port Royal

Immediately after Steedman's move, Captain Sylvanus Godon of the *Mohican* broke his ship off from his prearranged position. He steered instead to a spot to the northwest of Fort Walker, where his men could enfilade the fort from a stationary position. The rest of the column decided to follow the *Mohican*, leaving the *Wabash* and the *Susquehanna* to complete the circle and brave the gauntlet with the newcomer *Bienville*.

Du Pont kept signaling for his ships to return to their spots. For the better part of an hour his flags waved that command over and over. "How is it I can't get my signal obeyed, and my orders carried out?" he exclaimed at the height of the action.

Rear Admiral Steedman gave the following explanation for the movements of his vessel:

> *The* Bienville *was the leading ship in the flanking or starboard column. After the fleet had passed into Port Royal Sound, and as the* Wabash *was turning to pass out, Tattnall's gun-boats were seen approaching from the mouth of Skull Creek. The* Bienville *was at once pointed in that direction, and opened fire from the 30-pounder Parrott on the forecastle. The gun-boats replied with an ineffectual fire at long range. None of the shots reached her. A brisk fire was kept up from the Parrott gun, and as the shells began to fall among the gun-boats they turned and stood up toward Skull Creek. Here the* Bienville *could not safely follow them, as she drew over sixteen feet and had neither chart nor pilot for the channel; while Tattnall's river steamers, with their light draught and the familiarity of the officers with the waters, could retreat to a position where the* Bienville, *in following them, would almost certainly have taken the ground. Moreover, the* Bienville *was within hail of the flag-ship, and a word from the flag-officer would have sent her up Broad River had he desired her to assume the risk. After the second turn within the forts, the* Wabash *was proceeding slowly down, followed by the* Susquehanna, *when the* Mohican *and the vessels astern of her left the line and took up a position above Fort Walker. The position enabled these ships to enfilade the works; but the movement was a departure from the order of battle, and it continued, notwithstanding signals to close up from the flag-ship. The* Bienville *took her position astern of the* Susquehanna *and these two were the only vessels that followed the* Wabash *on her third circuit; or, to speak more precisely, on her second passage out and her third passage in, under the fire of the forts.*

Why the *Mohican* and the rest of the ships veered off to fight their own battle has not been adequately explained. Decades after the fact, Captain Ammen theorized:

Iron Tempest in Incessant Blast

Interior of Fort Beauregard after occupation. *Author's collection.*

> *Godon, who commanded her* [the *Mohican*], *was very excitable, and it may be on seeing a strange vessel ahead in his line, imagined that the well-planned attack had been transformed into a "free fight," and the best he could do was to serve his battery well from the most effective point he could take up.*

The traditional view of the battle—the one printed in the *Official Records* and in countless newspapers—shows the ships in the formation that was planned, rather than the one that occurred. The public at large was uninformed about this variance of the plan until Ammen published an account of the battle in 1883. Why the silence? Du Pont was well versed in the politics of navy service and had no wish to engage in an acrimonious letter-writing war with his subordinates or to waste energy arguing a pointless controversy. If the battle had unfolded another way, this may not have been the case.

Rodgers wrote to his wife another account of the battle:

> *Yesterday we had a fight which was described by the army in the ramparts as sublime. The fire of this vessel was awful. The flames leaped through her ports too quick for counting and the shot fell with the precision of target practice....Nothing General Sherman had ever imagined had ever equaled the terrible iron storm which so rained upon the fort. I looked carefully*

> with the glass at the fort during the action. Shells were bursting in the fort as fast as you would your fingers in playing upon the piano...During the terrible fire our ship apparently desperately near the battery was handled with the coolness of holiday sailors...The soundings were called regularly as the vessel was seen by them, close, closer to the battery...Signals were made continuously to the rest of the vessels for their guidance and not a single mistake was made...The balls and shells flew thick over our heads. The shells screaming like fiends. The balls with a roar and lower note than the rifle shells...admirable self-possession was shown in handling the vessel so nobly...The men at the guns were as cool as possible. In a word, it was a spectacle for an American to be proud of...I did some little things which seemed brave but which were really not so brave as standing on the bridge.

During the exchange, Rodgers cut away a spar and helped pull up a bundle of roping—the hawser—that was in danger of fouling the propeller. "This letter is egotistical," he continues, "but as we have the glory I hope you will not consider it out of place. When one writes to his wife he is permitted to be egotistical." In yet another letter about the Port Royal Expedition, he confided, "I have come to the conclusion that I am a good man in a battle."

Out on the transports, a solider watched eagerly:

> The rebels seem to like the **Wabash** better than any other ship...During the whole of the fight I could see shot strike the water, sending up a fountain in the air some 15 or 20 feet high. They would drop on all sides of some of the vessels, but not many seemed to hit.
>
> The second time the **Wabash** came round was well worth traveling a thousand miles to see. She looked like a cloud of smoke and flame so incessant a fire did she keep up...I counted 50 shells bursting at once in and close around it.

Fort Walker had so far taken the brunt of the attack; it suffered dearly under the enfilading fire. General Drayton commented, "This enfilading fire on so still a sea annoyed and damaged us excessively, particularly as we had gun on either flank of the bastion to reply with."

Colonel Wagner remarked:

> Most unfortunate for us was the mistake of the engineers, which I had pointed out before the battle, of having failed to establish a battery on the bluff which commanded our flank. The enemy having taken position in the mouth

Iron Tempest in Incessant Blast

> *of the creek exposed us to a raking fire, which did us the greatest damage, dismounting our guns and killing and wounding numbers of our men.*

Drayton's aide, Langdon Cheves, sketched a diagram for his wife of how the fleet's fire enfiladed the fort he was stationed in, stating that she "may conceive that we were in a pretty pickle."

Cheves also wrote her a descriptive account of the bombardment:

> *The discharges were almost a continuous roar; the scream of shot through the air so constant that it was sometimes not possible to distinguish them singly. It was on a large scale like the sound of a flock of birds swooping over head. Shells were bursting every second or two in the parade of the fort, in the traverses & parapet and at times the air was darkened with the masses of sand thrown up by their explosion. I suppose that nearly a dozen times I was covered with the harmless dirt shower.*

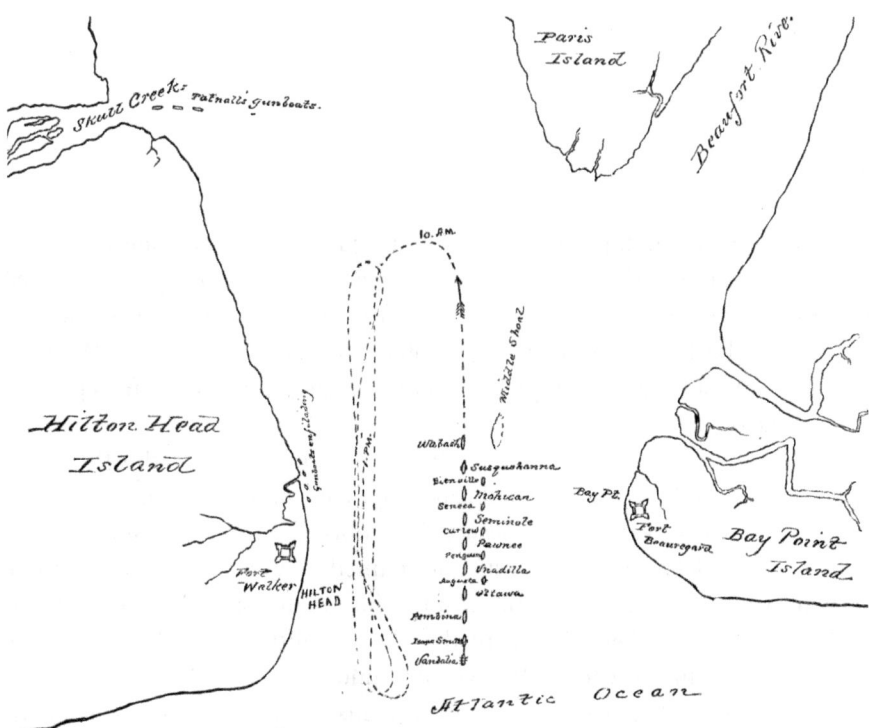

PLAN OF THE ATTACK ON FORTS WALKER AND BEAUREGARD, NOVEMBER 7, 1861.

Author's collection.

The Battle of Port Royal

Dupont's Round Fight (November 1861)

By Herman Melville

*In time and measure perfect moves
All Art whose aim is sure;
Evolving rhyme and stars divine
Have rules, and they endure.*

*Nor less the Fleet that warred for Right,
And, warring so, prevailed,
In geometric beauty curved,
And in an orbit sailed.*

*The rebel at Port Royal felt
The Unity overawe,
And rued the spell. A type was here,
And victory of LAW.*

Despite shells landing around him with such frequency, Cheves would escape the battle uninjured. There was one close call, however. He had set his officer's saber to the side while he was sitting behind a gun. A shell missed the gun but hit his sword, flinging the splintered hilt into his chest: "Without moving I put out my hand & picked up the damaged weapon." He kept it as a keepsake of the occasion.

At this point, several gunships outside of the column were steadily throwing fire into the fort, the shot and shell traversing the length of the fort. Arriving late on the scene was the *Pocahontas*. The storm and assorted mechanical problems had delayed the screw steamer named in honor of the Algonquian Indian princess. It was not until the morning of the seventh that the crew was able to get their bearings off of the Tybee Lighthouse in Georgia. From that landmark, they raced to Port Royal Sound.

Captain Percival Drayton was especially anxious to get there in a timely fashion. Percival's loyalty would be called into question should he not put in an appearance, even if it was due to circumstances out of his control. Another person of note serving with Percival was his executive officer, Alfred Thayer

Iron Tempest in Incessant Blast

Mahan, who would go on to be an author and influential naval theorist. On the route to Port Royal, the *Pocahontas* was almost delayed again. It spotted a ship that had all the hallmarks of a blockade runner. Although it was in a rush, the *Pocahontas* could not allow this illegal commerce to go on under its nose.

As fate would have it, it turned out not to be a blockade runner but a coal barge headed for Port Royal. Since they shared a mutual destination, and the *Pocahontas* needed to refuel its own depleted coal bunkers, the *Pocahontas* hitched the barge and towed it. At 10:00 a.m., the ship's crew could hear the sound of a cannonade. The sound carried down the waterways as far as seventy miles away to Fernandina, Florida.

The noise was the final impetus for Percival. With apologies to the captain of the barge, the *Pocahontas* cut loose its tow and headed toward the thunder of the guns at full throttle. It was noon when it entered the sound, following the new buoys. Percival quickly surveyed the situation and directed the ship to pass Fort Beauregard, throwing shells as it passed. It followed the lead of the other ships and took a place above Fort Walker, firing until the signal to cease was given. In the roughly two hours it was engaged, the *Pocahontas* fired seventy shells of various caliber.

On the third pass, the *Wabash* emptied its guns into a quiet fort. It received no reply. At 1:15 p.m., the *Ottawa*, one of the gunboats, signaled that the fort had been evacuated. For good measure, the *Susquehanna* delivered a broadside. The *Pembina* echoed the message of the *Ottawa*—the Confederates were fleeing.

The *Wabash* disgorged a small boat with Rodgers and a small escort of marines. Rodgers had brought two flags: a white flag of truce to parlay with the defenders, if they still remained, and the Stars and Stripes, if they did not. Seeing no Confederates there to meet them, Rodgers carried the staff bearing the red, white and blue banner and plunged it into the ramparts of Fort Walker.

✳✳✳

At 10:30 a.m. the Confederate gunners in Fort Walker could hardly stand. They were dead on their feet, exhausted from the laborious chores of loading and firing the guns and mentally fatigued from being exposed to such a heavy return fire. Seeing their plight, General Drayton left the fort and rode over a mile across the contested ground to fetch Captain Read and his men. Read's men were ordered in to prop up the fatigued men.

Drayton remained inside the fort himself until 12:30 p.m. Sensing an end, he turned command over to Colonel Heyward, with orders to hold out as long as they could, and left the fort a second time to gather infantry and the reserves.

The Battle of Port Royal

Mounting his white steed, Drayton and his aide joined the troops mustered at a location known as "Hospital No. 2." This was where he got news that a couple of small steamers were sounding dangerously close to the beach. This could only mean one thing: a prelude to a landing.

Knowing that he was going to be needed elsewhere, Drayton detached one of his aides with Captain Berry. Three companies of Berry's "Gallant Georgians" were to watch these boats and beat back a landing attempt if it came.

This crisis attended to, Drayton rode off with the rest of his staff to scour the island roads for stragglers. Reinforcements were trickling in, but these coastal roads could be difficult to navigate. No doubt some of them had simply lost their way to the front. While sweeping the roads, Drayton encountered an unexpected visitor just over a mile from Fort Walker. It was his superior, the department commander General Ripley and his staff. Drayton describes this meeting:

> *Saluting him, I inquired if he visited the island to assume command, and whether he wished to go back with me into the fort. He said no, but that he would return to Coosawhatchie to collect and bring back two or three regiments to my support. We then moved from under the fire of the ships to the shelter of some myrtles, where we could not be seen. I then stated to him the incidents of the morning; how the men had fought, that the day was going against us, and I was then collecting my forces for any emergency that might arise; and, if compelled to defend the island, it should be retained to the last extremity.*

The two parted, Ripley going back to the command center at the locality known as Coosawhatchie. Drayton returned to Hospital No. 2. He was informed that in the time he had been absent the enemy had ceased making soundings and had gone back to sea. Captain Berry was ordered to return from the beach. At two o' clock, Drayton noticed "our men coming out of the fort, which they had bravely defended for four and a half hours against fearful odds."

Colonel Heyward gave the following testimony explaining why he had retired from the fort :

> *About 2 p.m., finding the fire of our batteries had nearly ceased, I inquired of Major Huger where Colonel Wagener was. He informed me that the colonel had been stunned by the bursting of a shell, and that he (Major Huger) was then in command of the battery. On consulting with him it was determined that Mr. L. Cheves and myself (Mr. Cheves acting as aide to General Drayton) should proceed to the magazine and inquire into the state of the ammunition. On reaching the door we were met by Lieutenant Scanlan, who reported that*

there were about ten or eleven rounds for 32-pounders left. On returning and reporting this to Major Huger it was decided that, as we could light no longer with any hope of success, one or two guns should still be served slowly until all the wounded could be removed, and then to evacuate the fort.

Drayton started rattling off orders, deploying units here and there to protect the routes off Hilton Head and onto the mainland. Langdon Cheves and a comrade attempted a dash to the officers' quarters to retrieve some items before the fort was abandoned. They made it to the outside of the quarters, but the volume of fire was making any further delay here extremely dangerous. Cheves recalled that his fellow officer "suggested that we had better quit…& quit we did at the stride of men at urgent business."

But such an escape! It was a rush through the same fire that had only been prevented by our good dirt walls from pounding us to atoms…On the road we passed three or four men stark dead & two mangled wretches still alive.

General Ripley would not have to bother sending reinforcements. The defense had become a retreat.

※※※

The nineteen-gun Fort Beauregard had not received the volume of fire that its sister fortification, Fort Walker, had withstood, but it had endured a severe shelling. About thirteen men were wounded in the crossfire, two of them losing an arm.

Only five of its nineteen guns had the range to fire on the fleet as it circled round to Walker. The distinguished militia company Beaufort Artillery, under Captain Stephen Elliott, manned these guns with great skill but ultimately had little impact on the outcome of the battle. It was not long before the men in this fort noticed that something was wrong with Walker.

Captain Elliot offers the following exchange between himself and commander of the fort Colonel Dunovant:

"Captain Elliot, what is the condition of things over the river?"
"Fort Walker has been silenced, sir." Elliott replied.
"By what do you judge?" Dunovant inquired, likely casting a glance over at the location of the Fort, still shrouded in a haze of powder smoke.
"By the facts that the fort has been subjected to a heavy enfilade and direct fire, to which it has ceased to reply; that the vessels have terminated their fire,

> *the flag ship has steamed up and delivered a single shot which was unanswered, and that thereupon cheering was heard from the fleet."*
>
> *"Then, sir, it having been proved that these works cannot accomplish the end for which they were designed—that of protecting the harbor—you will prepare to retire from a position from which our retreat may readily be cut off, and which our small force will not enable us to hold against a land attack."*

Captain Elliot gave the orders; the guns were spiked and water casks were poured over the powder cache. An hour after Dunovant gave his command, the defenders of Fort Beauregard were retreating.

✳✳✳

Commodore John Rodgers left the flag in the ramparts for only a moment. He realized that it wouldn't be seen at such a low spot. He surveyed the island and determined that the highest point would be from a nearby structure, a military building of some kind that would later be known as the Pope House. The flag of the United States was hauled up; it snapped in the wind and presented itself to the fleet.

The reaction out on the transports was immediate. Charles K. Cadwell, serving in the Sixth Connecticut, recalls this moment:

> *The different bands on the steamers struck up the national airs, songs were sung, and cheer after cheer rent the air from thousands of throats, while the loud huzzas swept through the fleet like a whirlwind, and not a few prayers arose to the God of Battles for giving us such a signal victory.*

Another similar account states:

> *Hip, Hip, Hurrah! We see—we rub our eyes—is it really true? We see the American banner once more floating over the soil of South Carolina. All this time we were looking on, silent spectators of the scene. But now the harbor rings with the shouts of applause with which we greeted the great naval victory.*

Then, alluding to the earlier feeling that the navy had delayed too long, the writer added, "We forgot for a moment how slow Secretary Welles is, and how dreadfully slow are all the operations of the Navy."

Iron Tempest in Incessant Blast

Raising the flag over Fort Walker. *Author's collection.*

Copp captured this moment as well:

> *Still watching through the glass we saw a boat lowered from one of the warships, put out and row ashore. In a few minutes up went the Stars and Stripes over Fort Walker...Then the wild shouts went up from the fleet amid the waving of flags, the bands all through the fleet joining in the hurrah, and playing the "Star Spangled Banner," "Yankee Doodle," and other patriotic airs...It was the greatest sight of one's life, never to be forgotten by every soldier who witnessed it.*

The Battle of Port Royal was over.

CHAPTER 7

AVENGED IS SUMTER'S HUMBLED FLAG AT LAST

"Run for your lives, each man for himself." These were the orders given the bloodied defenders at Fort Walker. This was not verbal permission for a wild rout. Necessity dictated these orders. A mile-wide swampy area easily in range of the Federal guns had to be crossed before entering the relative safety of the woods. Crossing in organized military units at a measured pace would have invited annihilation.

In the woods, they would follow a narrow track, stretching close to six miles to Ferry Point on Skull Creek. These would be hard miles to travel for the fatigued, fought-out men, some burdened by wounds while others carried their wounded comrades to safety. Details of 4 men had been delegated to carry the seriously wounded in taut blankets serving as stretchers. At the end of the road, their makeshift transports waited at the docks. The exhausted men climbed aboard several idling steamers, lumbered onto the deck of one of Commodore Tattnall's ships or found a place on the planks of one of the large flatboats capable of holding up to 150 men each. The movement from Hilton Head to the mainland was done with as much speed as they could manage. Should Du Pont enter Skull Creek, they would quickly find themselves under Federal guns again.

Du Pont's decision not to dispatch gunboats into Skull Creek—which would have cut off the Confederate retreat—was a controversial one after the armchair generals began their analysis. Even those who questioned this lack of action had to admit that there were sound reasons for avoiding it: the channel was

Avenged Is Sumter's Humbled Flag at Last

intricate, Mr. Boutelle could not be everywhere and the Confederates could have fortified the points along the banks, a situation to be avoided, especially as darkness approached. Since Skull Creek remained open to the rear guard, those men who had covered the retreat of their comrades were able to escape becoming prisoners or casualties.

Over at Dr. Jenkin's plantation, located on Station Creek on St. Helena Island, the spectators rushed to their horses. A large crowd of civilians had gathered on the grounds of the coastal plantation for a view of the battle. When it was clear that the day had gone against their hopes, they hurried back to their homes to prepare for their own retreat. A reserve unit of militia had watched the battle with them. The civilians went one way and the militia the other way to aid their brethren streaming out of Fort Beauregard.

The only line of retreat from the Bay Point fort was across a strip of land known as the Narrows. At barely fifty yards wide and one thousand yards long, it was aptly named. The Narrows led to the main body of Edding's Island, referred to by Colonel Dunovant as "extensive swamp, entirely impenetrable save by a trail known to few."

Thanks to the request of a few days earlier, a dozen flatboats had been sent to ferry the men from Fort Beauregard to Dr. Jenkin's plantation. Slaves, pressed into service by their masters, poled the weary soldiers to safety. Lieutenant Johnson was later commended by his superior for his "valuable services rendered at the ferry across Station Creek." Ever gracious, Johnson was quick to share the credit with Private Thomas Chaplin.

Much was made of the Confederate retreat. The Federals were determined to make it a rout, some attempting to assuage their own disorganized rush from Bull Run. Especially galling were the reports of cast-aside weapons. Knapsacks and accoutrements of that ilk could be forgiven, but abandoned weapons raised embarrassing questions about Southern valor.

Captain Stevens, one of Sherman's officers, commented:

> *The enemy's camp bore witness to his panic flight; clothing, bedding, half-cooked provisions, even a rebel flag over one tent and a sword inside, and in another an excellent repast, with jelly, cake, and wine, were found abandoned.*

One of the crew members of the *Unadilla* remarked, "Our insulted flag was vindicated." The victory at Port Royal was a multipurpose salve, it seemed. Not only could it wash away the rout of Bull Run, but it also restored the pride lost at Fort Sumter. Sumter was avenged, many exclaimed. The crewman continued:

The Battle of Port Royal

I don't think you will be troubled any more with anything about Bull Run, for it was not a circumstance to the stampede that took place here. I almost think they are running yet. They left everything—clothes, muskets, revolvers, swords, all their camp equipage.

The Sixth Connecticut Infantry historian chimed in:

Those who succeeded in getting away alive must have beat a hasty retreat, for knapsacks, blankets, and rifles lay in confusion all around, and were found at almost every step for miles through the woods.

The *New York World* narrative on the battle contained an eyewitness report:

Over the meadow...were scattered knapsacks (some of which, singularly enough, were recognized as those which had been cast away at Bull Run), muskets, bayonets, cartridge-boxes, and broken vehicles, not camp wagons, but family carriages, which had been used to carry away the dead and wounded.

Drayton took time to address this issue in his official report:

The muskets captured by the enemy, with the exception of some ten or fifteen, were those left in the fort, shattered by shot and shell, others left in camp belonging to men on sick leave, or those engaged in heating hot-shot furnaces two days before the fight, and some boxes of arms which had been left on the wharf the night before the battle, belonging to the sick men of Colonel De Daussure's regiment, who had been left behind...which could have been saved, along with a box of swords, if the Captains of the steamers had not refused to take them aboard when directed to do so.

Colonel Wagener offered another reason why the Federals may have found so many weapons:

Under the circumstances of our retreat nothing whatever could be saved by the men. They had been working at the guns in most cases in shirt sleeves; the sand had covered their knapsacks and muskets, sometimes two or three feet deep, and very few arms were therefore brought off and very few knapsacks and clothing saved.

Wagener implored the state to step in to care for these men, who were now "entirely destitute."

Avenged Is Sumter's Humbled Flag at Last

Colonel Dunovant accounted for the items found in Fort Beauregard by stating that the wild condition of the island on which the fort was situated and the difficult path of retreat precluded the

> *possibility of transporting baggage of any kind beyond what could be borne on the shoulders of the men. Of the character of the route and the consequent impractiablity of transportation I had been fully advised, and therefore did not undertake the removal of camp equipage stores, or heavy baggage. Nor did I think it prudent to destroy by fire, inasmuch as the retreat was at best of doubtful feasibility, and the nature of the movement would have been entirely revealed to the enemy.*

Despite these handicaps, Dunovant was adamant, "no soldier threw away his arms."

Only after the navy and the marines had staked out their trophies was the army permitted to come ashore. Eldridge Copp remembered:

> *Orders were immediately given for the landing of the troops; the transports weighing anchor one after another, steamed up the harbor in the direction of the captured forts.*
>
> *The enemy had retreated, and the landing was made without opposition, although with a great degree of difficulty, there being no wharves, and many of the launches and boats that had been depended upon for the landing of the troops lost in the storm.*

The historian of the Forty-eighth New York wrote, "Transports everywhere were discharging troops, and the harbor presented a most animated appearance." Federal Surgeon Weld expertly captured the chaotic nature of this event:

> *The scene on the beach where the soldiers were landing surpasses description. Guns going off, some fired by drunken marines and others by disorderly soldiers, men screaming, yelling and rushing about in perfect disorder made altogether a perfect pandemonium of the place.*

Some of the water-weary men were in for a final test of their patience. Several of the transports grounded, and they had to walk the rest of the way to solid ground in shoulder-high water, muskets and cartridge boxes held above their heads. Bonfires were built on the beach to warm these unfortunates. The sailors had already landed, and now it was the soldiers, reporters and civilian crews' turn to regain their land legs while exploring the forts. Copp of the Sixth Connecticut wrote:

> *Not until we landed did we know what dreadful havoc our shells had made: the sight beggars description…Every building near the fort was riddled by our shells while the tents were torn to shreds. Our surgeons provided for the wounded as well as they could with the means at hand.*
>
> *Many of the dead were literally torn to atoms, and some were half buried where they fell; guns were dismounted, army wagons smashed, and many fine horses and mules lay in heaps.*

A *New York World* reporter was entranced by the sight of a cotton field near the scene of action:

> *A beautiful cotton-field was near by, the bolls already burst and the long cotton hanging from them in the greatest profusion…unaccustomed to the sight of a field of ripe cotton the scene presented to me was one of unrivalled magnificence and novelty. It seemed as if a living mantle of snow rested upon a square of beautiful country, and undulated like the yellow grain in the gentle winds.*

Yet the battle had intruded upon this picture of natural beauty. In the same article the reporter noted:

> *The ground in every direction was ploughed into furrows and ridges by our shells and balls. The earthworks were honeycombed and torn in unsightly heaps, trees shattered in every direction, and long lanes cut through the pure white field of cotton.*

The journal of the *Vanderbilt*, written by a man identified only as H.J.W., read:

> *There was plenty of testimony regarding the destructiveness of our fire, not alone from the prisoners…but also from the very earth itself, where numerous deep and long furrows, caused by ricocheting shells, and fragments of jagged iron, in countless quantity, told mutely more effectively.*
>
> *Eight dead bodies, some shockingly mangled, were found within the fort. One was that of a young officer, whose legs had been shot away. There was a mangled arm in one place, half-buried in the sand, and another, near where the*

Avenged Is Sumter's Humbled Flag at Last

> *huge guns lay prone with their carriages shattered, were mangled pieces of flesh immersed in gore. I saw still other sickening things.*

In an expedition shortly after the battle, Weld recalled that he

> *came to a house about 2½ miles into the island where there were four rebels, three mortally and one severely wounded. One of them had just died under operation cutting his leg off and those horrible turkey buzzards could be seen hovering in the air over the house, smelling even so soon the dead man. It was a horrible sight and made me feel what war was.*

Lieutenant John Barnes, a naval officer who inspected Fort Walker soon after occupation, left the following grisly account of the Confederate dead near the toppled guns: "One or two dead…were lying, crushed out of all semblance of the form divine, a mere miserable dusty heap of gory clothes and flesh."

Confederate casualties were eleven killed, forty-eight wounded, three captured and four missing for a total of sixty-six. Barnes gives insight as to how their fallen enemies were treated:

> *Commander Charles Steedman, of the* Bienville, *himself a native of Charleston…assumed the task of interring the remains of those South Carolinians who had fallen. This was accomplished in as respectable a way as circumstances permitted, and the Episcopal burial service was read by the chaplain of the* Wabash.

The Federals had their own losses to attend to. Eight of their own were killed, and another twenty-three wounded. This number does not reflect the loss of those men or ships on the voyage down or the subsequent casualties that resulted from the battle. The history of the Forty-eighth New York Regiment mentions additional casualties caused by the voyage south: "The saddest memory will be that a number of the men who had the measles on shipboard had taken cold from exposure during the storm, and died after reaching Hilton Head."

Roswell Lamson, an officer aboard the *Wabash*, recounted the burial of those who were killed as a result of the battle:

> *This afternoon the saddest of all calls rang through the ship: "All hands—bury the dead." After the usual services on the gun deck a procession of boats was formed, the band leading, laying the dead march, then our first cutter containing the remains of the gun captain, his gun's crew and myself, his messmates*

followed, and the other dead seven men and one officer. As we left the ship the fleet lowered their flags to halfmast. We buried them in a beautiful spot underneath some large trees. Brave fellows, they will never answer to their muster again, but they died as American Sailors would wish to die, fighting for their Country. There were many wet faces as we fired the last volley over their graves. When my time does come I hope I may die as they have died, under the flag, and be buried within the sound of the ocean.

A *New York Times* reporter at the ceremony penned his own account of this same event:

The dead of the fleet were buried last evening, with considerable ceremony, in a pretty grove, not over a stone's throw from the fort, where lemon, orange, fig palmetto and other trees blend their branches peacefully. Seventeen boatloads of sailors from the fleet followed the bodies to their last resting-place, and after the prayers had been read a guard of marines fired a volley over each grave.

The fall of Port Royal caused much consternation. Mary Boykin Chesnut wrote, "I was sobbing to break my heart…Utter defeat at Port Royal." Charleston diarist

Federal graveyard at Port Royal. The bodies were later moved to the national cemetery in Beaufort. *Author's collection.*

Avenged Is Sumter's Humbled Flag at Last

Emma Holmes wrote on Friday, November 8, "The bad news from Hilton Head & Bay Point received this evening has cast a gloom over everything." This sadness soon transformed into fear. Another resident wrote:

> *There is great terror prevailing here and no preparations—neither troops nor defenses. I regard the city in hourly peril. I believe it could be taken in six hours…I believe they will have Charleston within thirty days.*

Savannah was also gripped with fear. A Georgia newspaper printed the following:

> *The capture of Port Royal created great excitement and considerable apprehension in Savannah. Families commenced packing up, and large numbers of females and children were sent from the city to the up-country.*

The Port Royal Experiment

Former slaves of CSA General Drayton. Many probably participated in the Port Royal Experiment.

The Port Royal Experiment is the term given to a humanitarian effort begun in South Carolina in late 1861 to determine if former slaves would be self-sufficient, to test the theory that free labor was more viable than slave labor and to prepare former bondsmen for emancipation and eventual citizenship in the United States.

The Confederate retreat after the Battle of Port Royal left the Federals in control of a large swath of South Carolina coastal area and the adjacent region, referred to as the Sea Islands, for the duration of the Civil War. As a result of the battle, most of the white residents, including the planter families, evacuated and left behind the vast majority of their slave workforce. On this newly vacated land, which counted roughly fifty plantation properties, there were an estimated eight to ten thousand individuals who had recently been held in slavery.

Federal officials experienced grave concern over such a large number of slaves suddenly within their lines. Part of the concern was humanitarian—with the traditional social structure upset and a large Federal force garrisoning in the area, there was the potential for a severe shortage of food, medicine and clothing. Another issue stemmed from political considerations. President Lincoln's government was not yet ready to take the step of *emancipation, for fear of public dissent, but neither did it wish to return the slaves to their masters, where their labor could be exploited to aid the Confederate war effort. As a result, the decision was made to follow a precedent set earlier in the Civil War, and the abandoned slaves were declared "contrabands of war" or simply "contrabands." Another concern was financial—at the time of the Federal occupation a sizable crop of Sea Island cotton, a lucrative commodity denied Northern business since the outbreak of hostilities, was currently in harvest. An attempt to salvage the cotton and return the profit to the government coffers had to be made. The U.S. Department of the Treasury, headed by Secretary Salmon P. Chase, was given jurisdiction over matters relating to abandoned enemy property and thus over the contrabands and cotton.*

In late 1861 and early 1862, Secretary Chase sent several treasury agents into the region to assess the contraband situation and attend to the cotton interest. The capture of Port Royal and the plight of the slaves had made national news. Fearful for the slaves' welfare, a New York American Missionary Association sent its own representative to gather information. After receiving suggestions from these various parties, Chase decided to back a cooperative venture between the government agencies and Boston and New York philanthropic organizations. The contrabands were placed back in the fields, tasked with harvesting the Sea Island cotton and provided with wages for their labor. The Federal officials' focus was on the cotton crop, while the civilian volunteers agreed to provide such services as public education. Both sectors would continue to supply material necessities as they were able.

In March 1862, a steamer transported the first wave of Northern volunteers into the area; they were from Boston and New York and were called "Gideonites" by the Federal soldiers. Although this was meant as a derogatory term, the name has become nearly synonymous with their goodwill efforts. With limited resources and limited support, these volunteers began to establish or organize for the contrabands free school and churches, issue supplies or serve as advisors to plantation communities.

One month later, a Philadelphian contingent of Gideonites arrived, among them Laura Towne, who would reside permanently in the area and found the Penn School. Other Gideonites followed, including Charlotte Forten, the first Northern African American schoolteacher to come south to educate the Port Royal slaves. On January 1, 1863, the Emancipation Proclamation went into effect on the Sea Islands, but for former slaves who were already involved in the Port Royal Experiment, conditions did not change significantly. Perhaps the most notable difference was that the term "contraband" was finally dropped and replaced with "freedmen."

Shortly after Emancipation, the plantation land in the region was officially seized by the Federal government for nonpayment of taxes. Many of those who had supported the Port Royal Experiment lobbied the government to institute a program that would carve up these abandoned plantations into smaller plots, which would then be sold at a reduced rate to

Avenged Is Sumter's Humbled Flag at Last

> *freedmen families. Instead, much of the plantation lands, numbering over 100,000 acres, were sold to private Northern investors, leaving only slightly more than 34,000 acres for purchase by the freedmen.*
>
> *In March 1865, as the Civil War came to a close, the Bureau of Refugees, Freedmen and Abandoned Lands, simply called the Freedmen's Bureau, was established, superseding the agencies running the Port Royal Experiment. Former officers of the experiment found that they were in a unique position to lend their skills and experience to this new agency and joined its ranks, many staying on until the disbanding of the Freedman's Bureau in 1872.*
>
> *Although there were difficulties and setbacks, the Port Royal Experiment was ultimately deemed a success and was referred to later as a "Rehearsal for Reconstruction." Interaction between the former slaves and the civilian and military agencies helped to dispel negative cultural stereotypes. In their diaries and letters home, the Gideonites remarked at the intelligence and natural ability exhibited by their students. Despite serious cultural misunderstandings and episodes of graft from unscrupulous businessmen or outright abuse from Federal soldiers, the contrabands worked diligently and efficiently, transitioning easily into the role of freed citizens.*

Another Savannah paper remarked, "You would be surprised…to see how deserted our town is. The church today looked as it does in yellow fever time."

Fireworks popped overhead the night of November 9. The navy bands played spritely patriotic tunes to accompany the pyrotechnic display. The last time most of the men had seen fireworks had been during the storm, when the illuminating rockets were sent up in alarm from the decks of troubled ships. Lighting the sky in celebration was far more preferable. After the first few days on shore, when the boats had been unloaded and preliminary defensive measures had been taken, it had been expected that the campaign into South Carolina or Georgia would begin in earnest.

It was expected that the Federals would begin a series of campaigns against Charleston and South Carolina from their new stronghold. Few military conquests would come from the capture of Hilton Head and Beaufort. General Isaac Stevens sheds light on this decision:

> *Immediately after landing, General Sherman held a conference with his general officers as to undertaking an offensive movement. The enemy was evidently*

The New Commander

ROBERT E. LEE

The Department of South Carolina, Georgia and East Florida welcomed its first commander on the evening of November 7, 1861, the day of the Battle of Port Royal. No one envied the situation he inherited. Resources were stretched thin before the successful Federal lodgment in South Carolina. Driving out these invaders would be the ideal solution, but reality dictated a holding pattern at best. Jefferson Davis's choice to put Robert E. Lee in charge of this dire situation did not elicit much enthusiasm from the public. Lee's father, Henry "Light Horse Harry" Lee, was a bona fide hero of the American Revolution and better known to South Carolinians. Robert E. Lee had hardly lived up to his father's reputation in the minds of many in the Palmetto State. He had served gallantly in the Mexican-American War, but his service in the Confederate military up until this time was viewed as lackluster. Out in what was to become the loyal Union state of West Virginia, forces under Lee's supervision had been soundly defeated. Newspapers took to calling him "Evacuating Lee" and "Granny Lee."

Lee summarizes his first briefing on the Port Royal situation on November 9, 1861, as follows:

> On the evening of the 7th, on my way to the entrance of Port Royal Harbor, I met General Ripley, returning from the battery at the north end of Hilton Head, called Fort Walker. He reported that the enemy's fleet had passed the batteries and entered the harbor. Nothing could then be done but to make arrangements to withdraw the troops from the batteries to prevent their capture and save the public property. The troops were got over during the night, but their tents, clothing, and provisions were mostly lost, and all the guns left in the batteries.

Avenged Is Sumter's Humbled Flag at Last

Lee went quickly to work to try to minimize the damage done by the loss of Port Royal. He set up headquarters at nearby Coosawhatchie and began arranging his department. Utilizing the wisdom of his subordinates like General Ripley, Lee formulated a policy of assembling troops at crucial junctures between the Savannah and Combahee Rivers. Their job was to shield Charleston and Savannah by protecting the vital railroad that ran between the two coastal cities. This would not be a static defense of simply sitting in harbor forts waiting to be attacked or hunkering in innumerable bastions along the railroad. Instead, this would be a highly mobile force—the very thing they were protecting was part of their arsenal. Rail cars would transport reinforcements to and from threatened points. Cavalry screens would patrol potential landing sites to sound the alarm. Clustered around the railroad was a thin line of smaller earthen forts, garrisoned with troops ready to either enact a stalling action or rush to another point of attack.

Four months later, Lee and his subordinates had a solid defensive system in place. They had been fortunate that no serious push, besides the skirmish at Port Royal Ferry, had been attempted by the Federals in Port Royal. A March 2 letter to his daughter, Annie Lee, gives a cautiously optimistic opinion of their efforts:

> I have been doing all I can, with our small means and slow workmen, to defend the cities and coast here. Against ordinary numbers we are pretty strong, but against the hosts our enemies seem to bring everywhere, there is no calculation. But if our men will stand to their work, we shall give them trouble & damage them yet.

The very day he penned this letter he received a telegram from President Davis. It requested his presence in Richmond, another place being threatened by a massive Federal advance. On June 1, 1862, Lee was appointed commander of what would become the Army of Northern Virginia. Although his tenure as department commander had been brief, it had been significant. The work begun by Lee in late 1861 would hold, against the odds, until the winter of 1865.

> *demoralized, and either Charleston or Savannah might fall before a sudden dash, and offered a tempting prize. But the general opinion was that a movement upon either involved too great risks, and that the first duty was to fortify and render absolutely secure the point already gained.*

Stevens claimed that he alone dissented from this view—perhaps this was true among the generals, but certainly many in the lower echelon wondered when they would move against other targets. Instead, they dug in. Copp wrote:

> A long line of earthworks was thrown up by the troops for protection from any advance that might be made. While we remained at Hilton Head we became very proficient with the shovel and pick, and for a time our muskets became rusty but the same could not be said of our shovels.

Naval Officer Davis was much harsher:

> The Navy had done its work slowly and cautiously, and, on the whole, successfully, while the army did practically nothing but sit down and hold the sea island which the navy had captured for it.

Du Pont tried to be more diplomatic in his assessment:

> There is no question now, both Savannah and Charleston could have been taken without loss *after our blow here*, as easy as Washington after Bull Run by the rebels—but then delays seem inherent on both sides. I do not blame the generals.

There were feints at the Battle of Port Royal Ferry in 1862, the Battle of Pocotaligo and in Secessionville, as well as other victories like the capture of Fort Pulaski, but for the most part the Federals roosted for the rest of the war in Hilton Head. The area's primary use was as a blockading and supply station for ships and troops serving in the theater.

Much labor and material were spent turning the Hilton Head area into a massive military installation. A floating depot with some facilities on Bay Point and St. Helena Island served as the naval depot. Hilton Head Island itself became an installation—Headquarters for the Department of the South—with all of the logistical centers for quartermaster commissary, ordinance and assorted offices. Two years after the battle, another Federal soldier, Robert Stewart Davis, offered a descriptive account of the appearance of the area:

> It is June, 1863. We stand upon the Government pier at Port Royal… There is every evidence of military life around us. Looking up the pier, we see, clustered almost the beach of Hilton Head Island, the little village of Port Royal, with its long, low buildings all sporting canvas roofing, which glitters in the sunlight like a canopy of pearls…The pier is crowded with quartermaster, commissary, and ordnance stores; vessels are being loaded

Avenged Is Sumter's Humbled Flag at Last

THE BATTLE OF PORT ROYAL FERRY

Christmas 1861 was a dreary time for Confederates in South Carolina. Port Royal had fallen in November, and on December 11 a great fire burned a destructive swath across Charleston's streets. The fire was accidental and not directly the result of the war—a small comfort to the multitude who lost their homes, businesses or churches in the blaze. At first it had seemed as if there would be, if not silver, a slightly lighter lining in this oppressive storm cloud. The Federals had been content to entrench and patrol from their new post in Port Royal. This had given the Confederates the opportunity to organize and strengthen. An emplacement was built at Port Royal Ferry to watch and delay any further Federal movement. This emplacement, along with two other advanced positions on the Coosaw River and Seabrook Ferry, gave them a little bit of breathing room.

On December 19, a quartermaster ship, the Mayflower, *during a reconnaissance mission skirmished with the Port Royal Ferry position. An artillery shell had damaged the* Mayflower, *and musket balls had swept its decks. One soldier aboard was mortally wounded in the exchange. This minor victory was perhaps another point of light to hold up against the defeats of the last year.*

PORT ROYAL FERRY BEFORE THE ATTACK.

The Battle of Port Royal

It would provide scant comfort. The Federals responded to the attack on their ship with a combined assault. General Sherman wrote that the purpose of the ensuing action, or "dash," was to

> destroy the batteries which the enemy appeared to have erected on the Coosaw River for the obstruction of the navigation and the passage of that stream, and also to punish him for the insult in firing upon the steamer *Mayflower* on her recent passage through that stream for the purpose of sounding the depth of the channel.

The amphibious expedition led by Brigadier Isaac Stevens and Commander C.R.P. Rodgers overpowered the Confederate defenders and destroyed their earthworks at this site. The cost was two deaths, twelve wounded and one missing. The Confederates paid a higher toll, with eight dead and twenty-four wounded. Instrumental in winning this battle was the use of a new army signal system developed by Major Albert J. Myer. Several members of the newly minted United States Signal Corps were part of the Port Royal Expedition, and their skill at relaying commands with a system of flags and various lights was used to great effect at the Battle of Port Royal Ferry.

This success was not followed up, however. The Federals returned to Port Royal rather than advancing further. Their attention would turn instead to Fort Pulaski along the Georgia coast.

> *and discharged; steamers are arriving and departing, this from Fort Pulaski, that for Folly Island, tugs are screeching through steam-whistles as large as themselves; teams with "U.S." on them in big black letters, are waiting for their "turn" or rattling down empty to the base of operations, or dragging their slow lengths along under heavy loads of hay, army bread, and empty shell; details of soldiers work easily in the broiling heat, or listlessly sit upon box and barrel, waiting for a breeze to spring up; contrabands...are indulging in free-labor, interspersing their work with sly shuffles and weird plantation melodies; officers are shouting orders, and quartermasters riding hither and thither; the harbor is covered with vessels—every thing from a ship to a sloop is lazily riding at anchor on the scarce-heaving bosom of the tide; men-of-war are not wanting, but, like sullen sea-dogs, slumber in the midst of so much life, always ready, however, for action; above them all towers the* Wabash...*This is an interesting view; but would be more so if the sun were not so hot and the sand-flies hovered less thickly.*

As expected, there were differing opinions about the importance of battle. A Federal soldier declared:

Avenged Is Sumter's Humbled Flag at Last

SEASON OF PILLAGE

Securing the landing area and the forts was the first order of business. When no immediate danger was detected, the Federals turned their attention to a less reputable pursuit: looting. Post-battle adrenaline surge, greed and bottled-up hostility gave the ransacking a vindictive element. The military sites, nearby abandoned plantations and evacuated Beaufort all were victims. Physician William Lusk summed up the feelings of many of his brethren with his statement, "Here lived the Pinckneys, the Draytons, and other high-blooded Hidalgos, whose effervescing exuberance of gentlemanly spirit have done so much to cause our troubles."

Federal surgeon Weld lamented his inability to participate: "I was so busy most of the time I had no chance to get any plunder…Many of the marines got swords, pistols, guns, watches etc. from the tents." The higher-ranked officers seemed determined to put an end to this unsightly graft. Weld noted, "The general was going around stopping the men from plundering."

H.J.W., aboard the Unadilla, *offers a frank assessment:*

> Meanwhile as the troops landed, they scattered themselves about the encampment, apparently under no control of their officers, but possessed with one idea of plundering the property which the rebels had left…The soldiers were eclipsed, however, in their disgraceful deeds by the crews and some of the officers of the transports. These last, not content with securing a slight memento of the fight, filled their boats with trunks, muskets, and other "portable property" which they placed aboard their ships, then returned for more. It was painful to witness the destruction of clothing, which the ravagers trod under foot after they had obtained it from trunks that were broken open in their desire to find more valuable spoils. The free use of whiskey, which was found in abundance among the officers' stores, began to have its effects upon the men; and finally after some stringent measures had been resorted to, was some degree of order restored…I learned that the tars *[sailors]* who landed earliest obtained some splendid trophies. The most elegant was a sword…probably an heirloom.

H.J.W. also mentions the "large Confederate flag," which would become known as the Fort Walker flag (see sidebar in chapter 5).

The graft did not end at the forts and nearby camps. Homes in the countryside, plantation manors and even the town of Beaufort suffered as the Federals advanced. Lusk sarcastically commented:

The Battle of Port Royal

> And now we vile Yankee hordes are overrunning the pleasant islands about Beaufort, rioting upon sweet potatoes and Southern sunshine...The country for many miles around has fallen into the hands of our armies and unhappily, victors are apt to be ruthless in destroying the property of conquered enemies.

The chronicler of the Forty-eighth New York regiment recalled:

> We were marched about a half mile back from the shore, and went into camp in the midst of a cotton-field. Scouting parties were sent out over the island, and they captured horses, mules, chickens, pigs and everything they could lay their hands on, and divided the "eatables" between the different companies. That however, was not considered "stealing" but confiscating.

Newspaper correspondent Noah Brooks wrote about the effect this unseemly activity had on St. Helena Episcopal Church:

> This fine old church, I regret to say, has not been spared from the ravages of war, but shows the traces of the vandal hand upon it. An old English-made choir, has been disemboweled by someone, and the ivory of its keys has been forced off, it is a mute but eloquent witness to the ruthlessness of the soldiery who first landed in this quiet spot.

The Federals were not the only ones engaging in looting. There are numerous accounts painting the slaves, left behind by their masters, as culprits. Brooks recounted:

> The slaves, intoxicated with their sudden freedom, ransacked the houses of their proprietors, plundering and gutting the wardrobes of masters and mistresses...dancing upon the polished pianos or marble tables, feasting upon choice dainties...and "closing out, regardless of cost" the stores of the town.

This atmosphere could not go on indefinitely. Officers (those not engaging in it themselves) were horrified at this behavior and how their men were being portrayed in the

Avenged Is Sumter's Humbled Flag at Last

press. Orders circulated from the top with a view to squelching this licentious behavior. Lusk recalls the end:

> However, the season of pillage is almost over. Our camps are being well guarded, and the opportunities for the escape of straggling parties of marauders have ceased. Every effort has been made to check wanton excesses, and it has been made for a few days past the sole duty of the Aides to scour the country for the purpose of intercepting parties wandering about without proper authority.

The 7th of November, 1861, will ever remain in the history of the war as one in which a grand victory was perched upon the banner of the Union: when treason and rebellion received a blow from which they never fully recovered.

The *Charleston Mercury* did not argue the importance of the victory but sought to temper the loss:

The mortification of the disaster is lessened by the consciousness that our troops deserved success. What injury we did to the enemy, we do not know. Our firing was, of course, less efficient than theirs. Our troops were volunteers—theirs picked artillerists. Yet, it is very remarkable how few were killed or wounded, amongst our troops. This battle, in this respect, was very much like the battle of Fort Sumter [alluding to the April 1861 incident in which the only casualty of a sustained bombardment was a single Federal soldier]. *How many cannon could have been rendered useless, and yet so few of those who worked them injured, seems very marvelous. Our troops did their duty faithfully and bravely, and fought until to fight longer would have been sheer folly. Though encountering immense odds, no signs of cowardice marked their conduct. Officers and soldiers exemplified the ancient character of the State, and deserve our profound gratitude and admiration.*

Perhaps the most fitting tribute to this battle and to those who fell, from both the North and South, is the USS *Port Royal*. The second ship to bear this name, in honor of the 1861 battle, was christened in 1992 and entered United States Naval service in 1994. This *Ticonderoga*-class guided missile cruiser is made up of men and women not from one section of the United States but hailing from all over a country reunited since 1865. This ship is a visible reminder of the American lives lost at the Battle of Port Royal.

The Battle of Port Royal

Beaufort Occupied

Two days after the Battle of Port Royal, the Federal navy visited Beaufort; army troops did not get there until early December. "The visit," noted Lieutenant Ammen,

> brought to view an extraordinary scene. On the wharves were hundreds of negroes, wild with excitement, engaged in carrying movables of every character, and packing them in scows. As the gunboats appeared a few mounted white men rode away rapidly...A very beautiful rural town had been abandoned by all the white inhabitants, quite as though fire and sword awaited them had they remained.

Benjamin Lossing put this account of the capture in his history of the war:

> Beaufort, a delightful city...where the most aristocratic portion of the South Carolina society had summer residences, was entered, and its arms and munitions of war

Beaufort was abandoned by the Confederates after the battle and by the next month was occupied by the Federals. *Library of Congress.*

Avenged Is Sumter's Humbled Flag at Last

seized, without the least resistance, and there being, it was reported, only one white man there, named Allen (who was of Northern birth), and who was too much overcome with fear or strong drink to give any intelligible account of the affairs there.

Davis, of the Wabash, *also ventured to Beaufort:*

When we landed we found a scene of desolation and ruin, in some place almost too painful to dwell upon. The only people we saw were the negroes, standing at the corners or wandering through the streets, looking on in amazement. The absence of population in a compact, fresh, well-built town was in itself a most melancholy sight.

Although by all accounts abandoned, it was not until December that the Federals formally occupied Beaufort. It would become a popular resort for soldiers and sailors on leave for the rest of the war and served as home to numerous Federal facilities.

Selected Bibliography

Browning, Robert M. *Success Is All that Was Expected: The South Atlantic Blockading Squadron During the Civil War.* Dulles, VA: Brassey's Inc., 2002.

Cadwell, Charles K. *The Old Sixth Regiment: Its War Record, 1861–5.* New Haven, CT: Tuttle, Morehouse and Taylor Printers, 1875.

Carse, Robert. *Hilton Head Island in the War-Department of the South.* Columbia, SC: State Publishing, 1981.

Copp, Elbridge. *Reminiscences of the War of the Rebellion, 1861–65.* Nashua, NH: The Telegraph Publishing Co., 1911.

Davis, Charles Henry. *Life of Charles Henry Davis, Rear Admiral, 1807–1877.* Boston: Houghton Mifflin, 1899.

Eldredge, Daniel. *The Third New Hampshire and All about It.* Boston: E.B. Stillings and Co., 1893.

Hayes, John Daniel, ed. *Samuel Francis Du Pont: A Selection from His Civil War Letters.* Vol. 2. Ithaca, NY: Cornell University Press, 1969.

Holmes, Emma. *The Diary of Miss Emma Holmes, 1861–1866.* Baton Rouge: Louisiana State University Press, 1994.

Holmgren, Virginia C. *Hilton Head, A Sea Island Chronicle.* Hilton Head, SC: Hilton Head Island Publishing Company, 1959.

Johnson, Robert Erwin. *Rear Admiral John Rodgers, 1812–1882.* Annapolis, MD: United States Naval Institute, 1967.

Jones, Katherine. *Port Royal Under Six Flags.* New York: The Bobbs-Merrill Co., 1960.

Selected Bibliography

Lossing, Benjamin J. *Pictorial History of the Civil War in the United States of America.* Vol. 2. Hartford, CT: T. Belknap, 1870.

Lowe, William. "Big Gun Bombardment of Port Royal." *America's Civil War Magazine* (January 2001). Available online at www.historynet.com/battle-of-port-royal.htm/7>.

Lusk, William Thompson. *War Letters of William Thompson Lusk.* New York: 1911.

McPherson, James M., and Patricia R. McPherson. *Lamson of the Gettysburg.* New York: Oxford University Press, 1997.

Merrill, James M. *The Rebel Shore: The Story of Union Sea Power in the Civil War.* N.p., 1957.

Reed, Rowena. *Combined Operations in the Civil War.* Annapolis, MD: Naval Institute Press, 1978.

Rowland, Lawrence, Alexander Moore, and George C. Rogers Jr. *The History of Beaufort County, South Carolina.* Vol. 1, *1514–1861.* Columbia: University of South Carolina Press, 1996.

Soley, James Russell. *Sailor Boys of '61.* Boston: Estes and Lauriat, 1888.

United States Naval War Records Office. *Official Records of the Union and Confederate Navies in the War of the Rebellion.* Washington, D.C.: Government Printing Office, 1894–1922.

Wilson, James Harrison. *Under the Old Flag.* New York: D. Appleton and Co., 1912.

Wyllie, Arthur. *The Union Navy.* Lulu.com, 2007.

www.ingramcontent.com/pod-product-compliance
Lightning Source LLC
Chambersburg PA
CBHW060812100426
42813CB00004B/1039